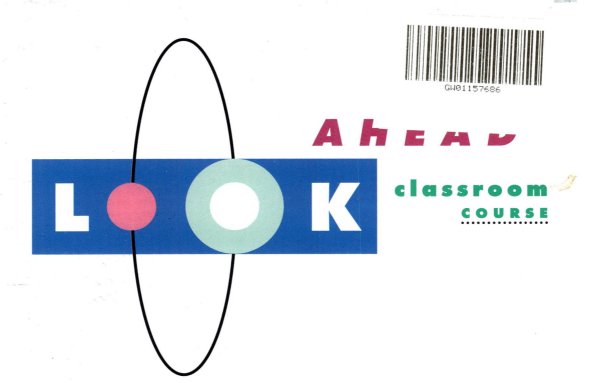

STUDENTS' BOOK 2

ANDY HOPKINS

JOCELYN POTTER

Look Ahead: a partnership between

 BBC English

 The British Council

 University of Cambridge Local Examinations Syndicate (UCLES)

 Longman ELT

 with the cooperation of the Council of Europe

	UNIT TITLE	PAGE	VOCABULARY AREAS	GRAMMAR
	Welcome !	6	The topics in this book	
1	At the weekend	8	Interests and hobbies Leisure activities Housework	Present simple/present progressive Question: *How often?* Adverbs of frequency *Would like* + infinitive with *to* Stative verbs
2	Doing new things	16	Languages Countries Adult education classes Times, dates, days, months Money Life changes	*Going to* + infinitive *Can/can't, could/could(n't)* + infinitive Adverbs: *very well, a little, not at all* *Like/enjoy* + *ing* *Want/would like* + infinitive with *to* Past simple
3	Planning a trip	24	Means of transport Travel	Comparative adjectives (+ *er* and *more*) Comparative adjectives (irregular forms) *Prefer* + *ing* Modal: *will* for decisions *I'll* + infinitive for promises *Let's* + infinitive
	Progress check 1	30		
4	Shopping for clothes	32	Clothes Clothes sizes	Adjective order *Too* + adjective *Not* + adjective + *enough* Superlative adjectives (*-est, most* and irregular forms) Comparative adjectives (irregular forms)
5	The rules of the road	38	Traffic rules and road signs Parts of a motorbike Problems on the road	*Can/can't* + infinitive *Have to/don't have to* + infinitive *Had to/didn't have to* + infinitive
6	How things work	44	Strange inventions Machines and equipment Controls	Imperatives Sequence words: *first, then, next* *For* + *ing* Phrasal verbs and position of object pronouns
	Progress check 2	50		
7	Getting around town	52	Waxworks Taxis Tipping Means of transport Times and distances Maps and directions	Adverbs of manner (*-ly* and irregular forms) Questions: *How far/long/much/often?*
8	Cooking a meal	58	Supermarkets Food and household goods Prices	Indirect (polite) questions Questions: *How much/How many/What kind?* Countable and uncountable nouns *Some, any, a lot of, (not) much, (not) many*

FUNCTIONS	READING/WRITING	COMPARING CULTURES
Giving/justifying opinions Giving reasons Talking about routines Talking about frequency	R: Articles about unusual interests R: Notices advertising future events R: Article about collecting phone cards W: Paragraph about an unusual hobby	Leisure activities
Talking about intentions Giving reasons Talking about ability Describing experiences Expressing feelings	R: Community centre prospectus R: Texts about childhood experiences R: Article about a child prodigy R: Text about vocational education W: Sentences about childhood W: Letter inquiring about a training course	Languages Community education
Making comparisons Giving invitations Making decisions for the future	R: Article about fear of flying R: Train timetable R: Article comparing train and plane travel W: Paragraph about travel plans	Means of transport
Describing and buying clothes Describing and asking about problems Talking about clothes sizes	R: Article about choosing clothes R: Article about a model W: Paragraph about seasonal clothes W: Paragraph about favourite clothes	National costumes
Talking about what is possible or permitted Talking about rules and obligations Explaining a problem	R: Articles about problems on the road R: Article about a traffic police officer W: Article about experiences on the road	Traffic laws
Talking about function Giving instructions Explaining how things work Making offers	R: Instructions for the use of an invention R: Text about video cameras R: Article about a stuntman W: Instructions for the use of an invention W: Description of a stunt	Video cameras
Describing manner Giving directions Talking about distance, time and frequency	R: Text about Madame Tussaud's R: Articles about journeys to work R: Boat trip brochure W: Postcard home	Taxis Tipping
Asking indirect (polite) questions Asking about price, quantity and means of payment Saying what you think Agreeing/disagreeing	R: Texts about food likes and dislikes R: Article about vegetarianism R: Restaurant advertisements W: Paragraph about eating habits W: Paragraph about vegetarianism	Food

	UNIT TITLE	PAGE	VOCABULARY AREAS	GRAMMAR
9	In the country	64	Locations Country and city life Pets	Modal: *should* + infinitive Tag questions
	Progress check 3	70		
10	Describing things	72	Lost property Qualities and features of objects	Indefinite pronouns and adverbs: *someone, anywhere*, etc. Questions: *What colour/shape? How big/heavy?* *Be made of* Possessive pronouns: *mine, yours*, etc.
11	You and your body	80	Parts of the body Illnesses Accidents Body language	Present perfect simple: *have/has* + past participle Adverb: *just*
12	People's lives	88	Individual achievements Life changes Periods of time	Adverbs used with the present perfect simple: *ever, never, for, since* Superlative adjectives used with the present perfect simple
	Progress check 4	94		
13	Things going wrong	96	Accidents and disasters Emergency and counselling services Problems and solutions	Present perfect/past simple contrast Reported statements Adverb: *ago* Reported questions *Ask + if, what, how,* etc
14	Celebrations	102	Celebrations Congratulations Parties Speeches and toasts	Adverbs used with the present perfect simple: *yet, already*
15	In the future	108	Means of prediction Weather and weather forecasts Problems and solutions	Modal: *will* + infinitive for prediction Adverbs: *perhaps, probably, definitely, certainly* *Less, least* First conditional: *if . . .*
	Progress check 5	114		
	Exercises for Student B	116		
	Grammar reference	123		

FUNCTIONS	READING/WRITING	COMPARING CULTURES
Talking about location Asking for and giving opinions Making comparisons Checking information	R: Article about travellers R: Article about pets R: Letter to a newspaper R: Article about city children W: Letter about your local area W: City code	Pets
Describing objects and clothes Talking about shape, colour, size, weight and material	R: Article about lost property R: Descriptions of objects and clothes R: Personal advertisements R: Extract from a play W: Sentences describing objects W: Description of clothes	Second-hand objects
Advice and suggestions Talking about illness Asking about problems Talking about events in the recent past	R: Emergency procedures R: Dance school brochure R: Article about a dancer W: Sentences describing accidents W: Expanding a text from notes	Body language
Describing people and jobs Talking about experiences in the indefinite past and past situations that continue into the present Expressing regret Apologising	R: Articles about famous people R: Biography of a very old woman W: Biography of an old person W: Own CV	Ways of apologising
Reporting what someone said Talking about past experiences Reassuring and calming someone	R: Text about a student counsellor R/W: Police officer's report R: Text about a firefighter W: Paragraph about an important possession	Emergency procedures and counselling services
Wishing someone well Congratulating/toasting/thanking someone	R: Greetings cards R: Newspaper announcements R: Text about weddings R: Wedding invitation W: Letter about a significant life event W: Thank-you letter	Toasting
Predicting Expressing hopes for the future Stating consequences	R: Weather facts R: Weather forecast R: Problems R: Articles about weather forecasting W: Paragraph about options W: Weather forecast	Ways of predicting the future

Welcome!

Getting to know *Look Ahead 2*

1 Look at the pictures on this page. Guess the topics in this book.

2 Work in pairs and match the pictures with the unit titles.
Student A: Look at this page and describe each picture to your partner.
Student B: Turn to the contents chart on pages 2–5 and identify the unit title from your partner's description.

3 Discuss your answers with another pair of students. Do you all agree?

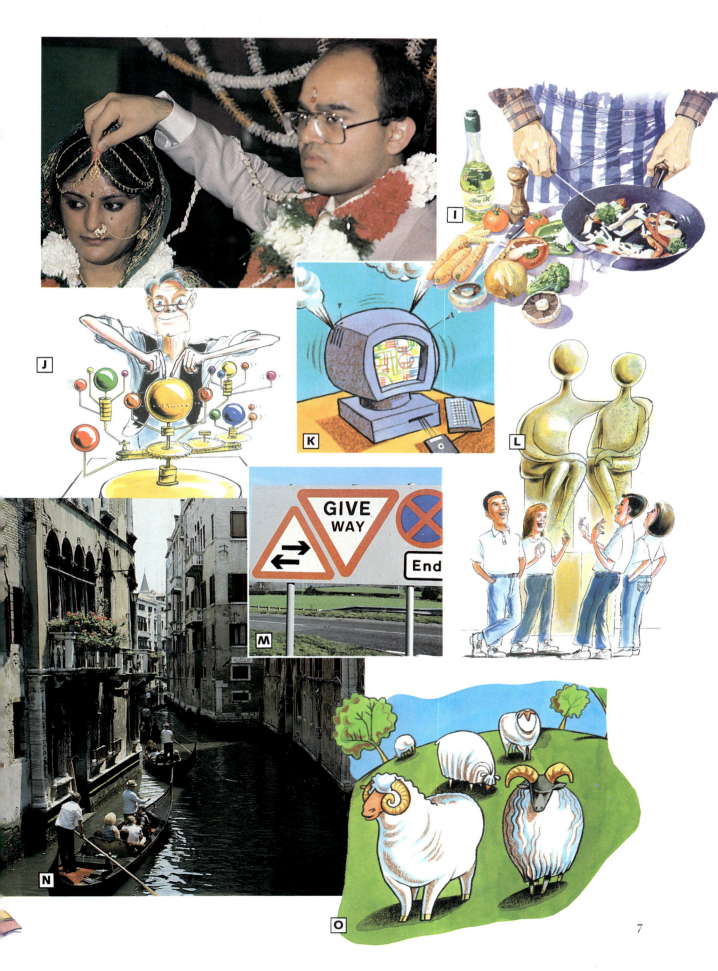

1 At the weekend

Special interests

Focus

- Interests
- Giving opinions
- Giving reasons
- Present simple/present progressive contrast
- *I'd like* + infinitive with *to*
- Conjunction: *because*

1 Read the magazine articles. Then look at the pictures and say what the people are doing.

1 Mark Coleman was born in New Zealand, but at the moment he is living in Britain. He is a leading member of the World Bungee Corporation. In his free time he jumps off bridges and hangs upside down with an elastic rope around his ankle. Bungee jumping started on Pentecost Island, near Australia, and a lot of New Zealanders now jump regularly. 'It's frightening at first,' Mark says, 'but it's very good fun.'

2 ROBERT HAAG is a 36-year-old American who is crazy about rocks. The 'Meteorite Man' collects and sells rocks from space. He lives in the mountains of Arizona, but he travels to the Andes mountains in Chile, to the Nile Delta in Egypt or to Australia to collect meteorites. He has the only piece of moon rock found on Earth outside Antarctica, and another piece that comes from Mars. 'I love the adventures, and the places that the rocks take me to. Every new rock is a challenge!'

3 Alison Peterson is a Londoner and works in the City of London, but in her lunch hour she forgets about the world of business. 'Take out three coloured balls and juggle for an hour every day,' she suggests. 'It's a very relaxing hobby. You can't think about your problems when you're juggling.'

I'm standing on a mountain with six other people, and we're completely alone. The world of heli-skiing is a silent, private one. You don't walk or queue for a ski lift; you pay a lot of money and take a helicopter. The helicopter leaves a small group of skiers, with a guide, at the top of a mountain, and the group skis down through the fresh snow. In Canada people return to the mountains again and again to enjoy the sport. 'I'm a dentist back home in Toronto,' says Mary Grove, one of my companions, 'and this provides the excitement in my life. I'm having a great time.'

2 Complete the chart with information from the articles.

NAME	COUNTRY OF BIRTH	HOBBY	REASONS FOR INTEREST
1 Mark Coleman	New Zealand	bungee jumping	good fun
2	.....	.....	.....
3	.....	.....	.....
4	.....	.....	.....

3 📼 Listen. In your opinion, which hobbies in the articles do these comments describe?

I think heli-skiing is probably dangerous.

1 It's dangerous.
2 It's boring.
3 It's frightening.
4 It's expensive.
5 It's fun.
6 It's exciting.
7 It's easy.
8 It's crazy.
9 It's relaxing.
10 It's cheap.
11 It's difficult.
12 It's challenging.

WORD STRESS

4 📼 Match the adjectives in Exercise 3 with their stress patterns below. Then listen again and check your answers.

1 o . .   2 . o .   3 o .   4 . o
   dangerous   expensive   easy   cheap

DISCOVERING LANGUAGE

5 Work with a partner. Read sentences 1–4 and say if the verbs are in the present simple or present progressive tense. Then match the sentences with the explanations, a) – d).

1 Alison works in London.
2 At the moment, Mark is living in Britain.
3 I'm standing on a mountain.
4 He often travels to Australia.

a) an activity happening at the moment of speaking
b) a regular repeated activity in the present
c) a present situation that has no time limit
d) a present situation that is only for a limited time

6 Work in pairs.
Student B: Turn to page 116.
Student A: You and your partner each have two pictures. Ask and answer questions and put the four pictures in the correct order. Use the verbs and nouns to help you.

A: *What's the woman doing in your first picture? Is she ... ?*
B: *She's ...*

| to jump | bridge | rope | to hang | boat |
| to wear | harness | ankle | to help | river |

7 Write what the woman above does each time she bungee jumps.

She wears ...

8 Write a sentence about each of the activities in Exercise 1. Say which activities you would like to try and give reasons.

I'd like/I wouldn't like to try bungee jumping because it's exciting/dangerous.

ENGLISH AROUND YOU

How do you say 'au secours' in English?

Frequency

Focus
- Leisure activities
- Housework
- Percentages

- Talking about routines
- Talking about frequency
- Expressing percentages
- Expressions of frequency: *once/twice/three times a year*
- Question: *How often?*
- Adverbs of frequency
- Verb/noun collocations
- Further practice: present simple

1 🔊 Rachel Hanson works as a research assistant for MAP, an advertising agency. At the moment she's interviewing a man about his weekend activities for a new magazine. Listen to the first part of the interview and say who the magazine is for.

2 🔊 Work in pairs. Listen to the whole interview.
Student A: Complete the chart with information about the man. Use the words on the right.
Student B: Complete the chart with information about the man's wife. Use the words on the right.

FRIDAY	
SATURDAY	
SUNDAY	

cinema   television   walk
Sunday lunch   exercise class
friends   sailing   restaurant

3 Work in pairs. Compare your answers to Exercise 2. Then say what the man and his wife do together and what they do alone.
A: *What does the woman do on Fridays?*
B: *She goes to an exercise class.*
B: *Does the man go to an exercise class on Fridays?*
A: *No, he doesn't. The woman goes to an exercise class alone.*

4 Put the adverbs below in order of frequency. Two adverbs refer to the same frequency. Which is more positive and which is more negative?

usually   never   sometimes   rarely   often   occasionally   always

5 Rewrite the sentences. Replace the phrases in italics with frequency adverbs from Exercise 4. Make any other necessary changes.
He goes swimming *every morning* before school.
He always goes swimming before school.
1 We play tennis *three or four times a week*.
2 I *only* go out *once or twice a month*.
3 They *don't* eat in restaurants *at all*.
4 She visits her grandparents *two or three times a year*.
5 He goes to the gym *almost every day* after work.
6 We go for a long walk *once or twice a week*.

DISCOVERING LANGUAGE

6 Look back at the sentences in Exercise 5 and at your new sentences. In the sentence below, where can you put:
a) an adverbial phrase?
b) a frequency adverb?
We (1) ..... watch a game of football (2) ......

7 Write these sentences again, using the word or phrase in brackets.
1 We watch a video. (every evening)
2 They go sailing. (never)
3 She plays badminton. (rarely)
4 He goes to the opera. (five or six times a year)
5 I cook Sunday lunch! (always)

8 🔊 Pronunciation. Listen. Notice the underlined sounds. Then listen again and repeat.
/sə/   On<u>ce a</u> year. Twi<u>ce a</u> month.
/zə/   Three time<u>s a</u> week. Four day<u>s a</u> week. Five time<u>s a</u> day.

9 Match each phrase with a picture.

1. do the shopping
2. do the cooking
3. wash the dishes
4. make the beds
5. sweep the floor
6. clean the bath

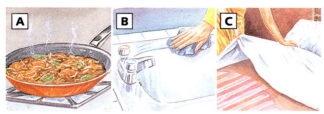

10 Ask your partner how often he/she does each task in Exercise 9. Then find out about other members of the family. Make notes.

A: How often do you do the shopping?
B: Occasionally. About once a month.
A: Who usually does it?
B: My mother. My father sometimes does it, and my brothers do it once or twice a year!

11 Write sentences about your partner's family, using information from Exercise 10.

Anna's mother usually does the shopping. Anna occasionally does it. Her father sometimes does it. Her brothers do it once or twice a year.

12 Work with a partner. Say which verb is used with each group of expressions.

do   make   go   play   watch   have

go for a walk/a swim/a drink

1. for a walk/a swim/a drink
2. television/videos/a football match
3. the guitar/the saxophone/the piano
4. to a party/a disco/a club/the cinema
5. tennis/table-tennis/badminton/football/basketball/baseball/volleyball
6. the shopping/the housework/the cooking/the cleaning/the gardening
7. dancing/sailing/swimming/riding
8. a meal/a barbecue/a party
9. the beds/a cake/a phone call
10. some exercise/some sport

13 Work in small groups. Write a questionnaire to find out what people do in their free time. Include ten activities. Ask other students about the activities and note their answers.

How often ...?

ACTIVITY	NAME/FREQUENCY			
	Clara	...	...	...
do/cooking	never			
do/sport	3 x week			
go/disco	Sat.			

Collect information from the other members of your group, and write sentences about the students that you interviewed.

Eighty per cent (80%) of the students in this class sometimes go to discos.

⟳ COMPARING CULTURES

14 Look at the chart. What does it tell you about the leisure activities of young British people?

Nearly seventy per cent of young people in Britain never go to youth clubs.

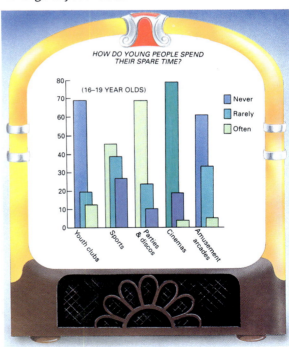

15 Is the information in the chart true for young people in your country? Which other activities are important?

In my country young people never go to youth clubs. They usually meet in cafés.

Around town

1 Look at the events advertised on the noticeboard. Say which event or series of events:
1 is for young teenagers.
2 is for unmarried adults.
3 is for animal-lovers.
4 is for serious walkers.
5 is for whole families who want to dance and have fun.
6 is to make money for developing countries.

2 Find a word or phrase in the advertisements that means:
1 you don't pay to go in.
2 more information.
3 to telephone.
4 children.
5 before the event.
6 without shoes.
7 things that people make with their hands.
8 presents to give to people.

Focus

- Further practice: leisure activities
- Justifying opinions
- Stative verbs
- *Would like* + infinitive with *to*

A RAMBLERS' CLUB
★★★★
Join us for a 10-mile country walk on Sunday, October 5th. Children and dogs welcome.
★★★★
Meet at the Market Square at 2 p.m. Strong shoes recommended.
★★★★
Call Jeff on 333865 for more information.

B COME TO THE
THIRD WORLD CRAFT FAIR
Saturday 24th October
10.00–4.00 Oxford Town Hall
Over 50 stalls – crafts, gifts, books, music, information, food
FREE ADMISSION

C **SINGLES SCENE**
Social club for single people looking for new friends. Ages 25–40.
ACTIVITIES INCLUDE:
parties · meals · walks · swimming · golf · bowling · concerts · theatre trips · night clubs · dances · days out
We meet every Thursday at Penn's Social Club, at 8.30 p.m. For further details call Daphne on 342798.

D YOUTH CLUB OPENING
☐ Are you between 12 and 16?
☐ Are you interested in joining a new Youth Club?
☐ Come along to the Clubhouse, Station Road on Saturday 26th September at 7p.m.
Further details: Carol Burns
Telephone 345110

E BAREFOOT BOOGIE
WILD FUN WITHOUT SHOES
Tickets £3 in advance, £3.50 at the door.
World's best music
Free drinks ✷ Delicious snacks
Balloons and surprises
Bring your kids – under 10s free!!
Saturday September 26th 8.00–11.30 p.m.
ASIAN CULTURAL CENTRE, Manzil Way
(near the Health Clinic)

F DEESIDE ANIMAL PARK
Fun Day
on Saturday Sept. 26th 10.00–6.00
Meet the animals
Rides · Displays · Entertainment
DEESIDE ANIMAL PARK, NEAR SOUTHDENE
Tel: 0244 636414 · ADMISSION £2

3 Work with a partner. Say which activities these people would like. Give reasons.

John collects old books and enjoys looking around markets.
I think John would like the Third World Craft Fair because he collects books and he likes markets.

1 Tina is twenty-six and moved to town last week. She doesn't know anybody and she wants to meet people.

2 Liz and Steve have two children of seven and twelve. Liz and Steve are interested in other cultures and they all like music.

3 Anne wants a place to spend the day with her little brother.

4 George and Tony are fourteen. They want to do new things with people of their own age.

5 Kate and Andy love the countryside, but they want to find new places to walk in.

4 Which events would/wouldn't you like to go to? Say why (not).
I'd like to go to the Animal Park because I love animals. I wouldn't like to join the Ramblers' Club because the walks are very long and I don't like walking.

DISCOVERING LANGUAGE

5 Look at these comments. Name the tense of the verbs in italics. Say what is unusual about the use of this tense here.
1 I'm enjoying myself. It's my first time here and I *love* this place.
2 I'm having problems with the language. What *does* 'boogie' *mean* in this advertisement?
3 Excuse me. I'm looking for Station Road. *Do* you *know* where it is?
4 What am I doing here? I'm here because I *want* to make new single friends.
5 Look at him! He's doing the walk, but he *hates* it.

6 Look at some other verbs that are not usually used in the progressive form. Then complete the dialogue with the correct present tense form of the verbs in brackets.

OTHER COMMON STATIVE VERBS (NOT USUALLY USED IN THE PROGRESSIVE FORM)
like   dislike   understand   believe

PAM: I (1) ..... (not believe) it! Rod, what (2) ..... you ..... (do) here?
ROD: I've got a job in this area and I (3) ..... (want) to meet people. It's difficult at work.
PAM: Yes, I (4) ..... (know). What (5) ..... your brother ..... (do) these days?
ROD: He's in Paris. He (6) ..... (have) a great time. He (7) ..... (love) France.
PAM: Oh, good. (8) ..... he ..... (understand) French now?
ROD: I (9) ..... (not know). You really (10) ..... (like) Steve, don't you Pam?
PAM: Yes, very much.

Development

SPEAKING

1 Look at the pictures of the Wheeler family and answer the questions.
1. Which country is this? How do you know?
2. Describe the family relationships in Picture A.
3. What are people doing in Pictures B, C and D?
4. How many rooms do you think their house has?

LISTENING

2 Listen and check your answers to Questions 3 and 4 in Exercise 1.

3 Listen again. Which of these activities do members of the Wheeler family do at weekends?
basketball   gardening   tennis   dancing
sailing   baseball   watch videos   barbecues
housework   go to the cinema

Now say what these people do:
1. the older boy   3. the whole family
2. the little boy

COMPARING CULTURES

4 Work with a partner. Which of the activities are also common in your country? Which are not common? What are the reasons for the differences?

READING

5 Read the article on the next page. Are these statements true or false?
1. A lot of British people collect telephone cards.
2. The first card for public telephones was British.
3. Each country produces one kind of telephone card.
4. Some cards cost a lot of money.
5. You need a lot of money when you start collecting cards.
6. It is easy to keep your cards at home.

SPEAKING

6 Discuss the article with your partner.
1. Do you find this hobby interesting? Give reasons.
2. Do you have phone cards in your country? Describe them and say whether they are attractive.
3. Tell your partner if you collect anything. List other things that people collect.

CALLING CARDS

Most British telephone cards are just plain green, but card collecting is becoming a popular hobby in Britain and collectors even have their own magazine, *International Telephone Cards*. One reason for their interest is that cards from around the world come in a wide variety of different and often very attractive designs. There are 100,000 different cards in Japan alone, and there you can put your own design onto a blank card simply by using a photograph or a business card.

The first telephone cards, produced in 1976, were Italian. Five years later the first British card appeared, and now you can buy cards in more than a hundred countries. People usually start collecting cards because they are small and light and you do not need much space for them. It is also a cheap hobby for beginners, although for some people it becomes a serious business. In Paris, for example, there is a market where you can only buy telephone cards, and some French cards cost up to £4,000. The first Japanese card has a value of about £28,000. Most people only see cards with prices like these in their collectors' magazine.

WRITING

7 Write a paragraph about an interesting or unusual hobby that you have or that you know about. Explain what it is and why it is interesting.

Summary

FUNCTIONAL LANGUAGE

Giving reasons
I like bungee jumping because it's exciting.

Talking about frequency
How often do you go to parties?
I go once a week/three times a year.
I often/sometimes/never go to parties.

Saying what you want to do
I'd like to go to the cinema.

Expressing percentages
Thirty per cent of young people in Britain go to discos.

GRAMMAR

Present simple (revision)
AFFIRMATIVE
I/you/we/they go.
He/she/it goes.
NEGATIVE
I/you/we/they do not (don't) go.
He/she/it does not (doesn't) go.
INTERROGATIVE
Do I/you/we/they go?
Does he/she/it go?

Present progressive (revision)
AFFIRMATIVE
I am ('m) staying here.
You/we/they are ('re) staying here.
He/she/it is ('s) staying here.
NEGATIVE
I am not ('m not) staying here.
You/we/they are not (aren't) staying here.
He/she/it is not (isn't) staying here.
INTERROGATIVE
Am I coming?
Are you/we/they coming?
Is he/she/it coming?

Adverbs of frequency
never   rarely   occasionally   sometimes   often   usually   always

**Common stative verbs
(not usually used in the progressive form)**
understand   want   know   dislike   like   love   hate

See the Grammar Reference section at the back of the book for more information.

2 Doing new things

Learning languages

Focus
- Languages
- Countries

- Talking about intentions
- Further practice: giving reasons
- Talking about ability

- *Going to* + infinitive
- *Want* + infinitive with *to*
- *Can/can't* + infinitive
- Adverbs of degree: *(very) well, a little, not at all*

1 How many of these languages do you recognise? Match them with the languages in the chart below.

2 🔊 Say these numbers. Then listen and repeat.
1,000   10,000   100,000   150,000   999,000   1,000,000

3 Work in pairs.
Student A: Ask and answer questions to complete the chart.
Student B: Turn to page 116. Answer and ask questions.

MOTHER TONGUE SPEAKERS (IN MILLIONS)			
English	.....	Chinese	1,000
Japanese	.....	German	100
Arabic	.....	Portuguese	135
Russian	.....	Spanish	250
Hindi	.....	Bengali	150

B: How many people speak Chinese?
A: One billion.

Now put the languages in order of the number of speakers.

🔄 COMPARING CULTURES

4 Work in groups and say what you know. Name:
1 a country where people speak Hindi.
2 two countries where people speak German.
3 three countries where people speak Arabic.
4 four countries where people speak Spanish.
5 five countries where people speak English.

5 Read what Alan says. Then write about your own first language. In which other countries do people speak it? Which other languages do people in your country speak as their mother tongue?

❝My first language is English. People also speak English in Australia, New Zealand, the United States, Canada, Ireland and a lot of other countries around the world. Some people in Britain have other mother tongues. These include Welsh and Scottish Gaelic, but also Punjabi, Bengali, Urdu, Chinese and European languages.❞

6 🔊 Listen and read. Rita Patel and Julia Marsh work at MAP Advertising. Julia is an account manager and Rita is a secretary. Answer the questions.
1 What does Rita want to study? Why?
2 When does she have time to study?

RITA: Oh, hi, Julia.
JULIA: Dreaming?
RITA: No, I'm thinking about evening classes.
JULIA: Evening classes?
RITA: Yes, I'm going to go to evening classes.
JULIA: Why?
RITA: Because I want to learn a foreign language. Japanese.
JULIA: Why do you want to learn Japanese?
RITA: Because I like Japan. And I want to do something new.
JULIA: Learning Japanese is going to be difficult.
RITA: I know. But I'm going to do it.

DISCOVERING LANGUAGE

7 Find examples of the structure *going to* + infinitive in the conversation in Exercise 6.
1 Do these sentences refer to the past, present or future?
2 When Rita says 'I'm going to go to evening classes', is this:
  a) a quick decision?   c) an offer?
  b) an intention?
3 How do we form affirmative and negative statements and questions with *going to*? Look at a) – c) below.
  a) I'm going to go to evening classes.
  b) Learning Japanese isn't going to be easy.
  c) When are you going to start?

UNIT TWO

8 Look at the chart and talk about these people's intentions for the future. Use a structure with *going to*.
James is going to paint his flat next week.

	NEXT WEEK	NEXT MONTH	NEXT YEAR
James	paint his flat	go to Edinburgh	not visit Ireland
Julia	begin a German course	not play at the jazz club	change jobs
Rachel and John	find a house	get married	not take a holiday

9 Write down five things you really want to do (e.g. go to university; get a job; live overseas; travel; retire). Ask your partner about his/her intentions. Then ask for reasons.
A: I'm going to get a good job.
B: Why are you going to get a good job?
A: Because I want to earn a lot of money.
B: But why do you want to earn a lot of money?
A: Because I'm going to buy a flat.
B: Why …?

10 🔊 Rita is at the community education centre. Listen and answer the questions.
1 Which languages can Rita speak?
2 Which languages can she write?

11 🔊 Now listen again. Correct the false statements.
1 Rita can speak French very well.
2 She can't write Hindi at all.
3 She can write a little French.
4 She can write English well.

12 Interview your partner and complete the chart about him or her. Use these phrases: *very well, well, a little, not at all*.
Which foreign languages do you know?
How well can you speak/write …?

	LANGUAGE	SPEAK	WRITE
First language	…..	…..	…..
First foreign language	English	a little	…..
Second foreign language	…..	…..	…..
Others	…..	…..	…..

13 Write about your partner. Use the information in your chart.
Lisa speaks French and Italian very well.

17

After school

Focus
- Times, dates, days, months
- Money
- Further practice: leisure activities

- *Like* + *ing*
- *Enjoy* + *ing*
- Further practice: *would like* + infinitive with *to*
- *Want* + infinitive with *to*

1 Look at the programme of courses. Find a course that interests you. Say why.

2 Find a course which is about:
1. writing good English.
2. learning a language.
3. using a camera.
4. the history of film.
5. cooking new dishes.
6. art.
7. playing an instrument.
8. staying in good shape.
9. preparing for college.
10. your family history.

3 Work in pairs.
Student A: Answer your partner's questions about the courses.
Student B: Turn to page 116 and ask your partner about the courses.

- B: When is the painting course?
- A: It's on Tuesday evenings.
- B: What time are the classes?
- A: Seven thirty to nine thirty.
- B: How long is the course?
- A: Ten weeks.
- B: And how much does it cost?
- A: Thirty-five pounds.
- B: Thank you very much.

COMMUNITY EDUCATION CENTRE

MONDAY evening

Foreign Cookery
Mrs L Bates
Watch, cook and taste. Dishes include Spanish, Indonesian, Mexican and Russian specialities.
5 weeks: £15

Cinema Studies
Mr T Green
Do you like watching films? Do you want to learn about the history of cinema? Try this course. The fee includes a trip to the Museum of the Moving Image in London.
10 weeks: £30

TUESDAY morning

Return to Learn
Ms S Askew
A friendly, informal course for adults with few or no qualifications who want to return to study. We provide free childcare at the Centre.
20 weeks: Free

Problems with writing?
Mrs L Lester
Learn to write with accuracy and confidence.
10 weeks: Free

TUESDAY evening

Painting in Watercolours
Mr P Love
Would you like to learn to paint? This course is for beginners only.
10 weeks: £35

Intermediate Italian
Ms T Battisti
Do you want to improve your Italian? We design courses for your special needs.
20 weeks: £100

WEDNESDAY morning

Jazz Exercise for Women
Ms T Baker
Keep fit and healthy to music.
20 weeks: £50

Family History
Mrs T Pearson
This course is for people who want to follow their family tree back through the centuries.
10 weeks: £25

WEDNESDAY evening

Photography
Mr L Webster
Learn to take better pictures and to set up a darkroom.
20 weeks: £55

Rock guitar club
Mr P Boss
Do you enjoy playing rock guitar? Come to the club to play and to listen to other guitarists. Bring your own instrument.
10 weeks: £50

TERM DATES

Autumn Term
Begins
Week 1: 21st September
Ends
Week 10: 30th November

Spring Term
Begins
Week 1: 11th January
Ends
Week 10: 22nd March

TIMES

Morning classes
10.00–12.00

Evening classes
7.30–9.30

DISCOVERING LANGUAGE

4 Work with your partner. Look at these questions from the programme opposite. Make rules about the verb forms that follow *like, enjoy, would like* and *want*.
1 Do you like **watching** films?
2 Do you enjoy **playing** rock guitar?
3 Do you want **to improve** your Italian?
4 Would you like **to learn** to paint?

5 Match each verb with one or more nouns.
watch television

watch   take   make   play   tidy   do   go   discuss   learn
wash   give

| the piano   English   television   computer games   politics |
| photographs   your room   dinner   homework   parties |
| the dishes   cakes   dancing   home   some exercise |

6 Stress and intonation. Listen and repeat. Which of the underlined words is stressed?

What do you enjoy doing?
What don't you enjoy doing?

Now ask these questions. Then listen and check with the cassette.
1 What do you like eating for breakfast? What don't you like eating?
2 What do you like watching on TV? What don't you like watching?

7 Look at the examples, then ask and answer questions about the people below.

(you/enjoy?) *What do you enjoy doing in the evening?*
– television   *I enjoy watching television.*
(you/not like?) *What don't you like doing?*
– my room   *I don't like tidying my room.*
(you/would like?) *What would you like to do after class?*
– dancing   *I'd like to go dancing.*

(he/enjoy?)
– the piano
– politics
(he/not like?)
– dinner
– the dishes
(he/would like?)
– home

(she/enjoy?)
– English
– photographs
(she/not like?)
– parties
– cakes
(she/would like?)
– some exercise

8 Ask your partner the questions in Exercise 7. Make notes and then write about your partner.
Paola enjoys ...

9 Read the questions. Then listen to an interview with the manager of a community education centre and make notes.
1 How many days a week is the centre open?
2 How many students use the centre?
3 How old are they?
4 Which are the most popular classes?
5 What other classes does the centre offer?
6 Where are the students from?
7 Why do they go to classes?

COMPARING CULTURES

10 Work with your partner. Discuss these questions.
1 Are there community education centres like this in your country?
2 What kind of people go to them? Do you go?
3 What courses can you do there?
4 Are the courses in the day or in the evening?

Young lives

1 🔊 **Listen and read.** Five people are describing new experiences that they had when they were young. Match the descriptions with the pictures.

1 Rosie: Oh, I hated it. I was five years old, very small and shy. My mother took me inside and there were a lot of other children. Did I cry? Well, I certainly cried when she left and I was unhappy all day. I felt awful.

2 Alan: My parents were worried about moving, but I wasn't. I was very excited. Of course, when we moved I lost some of my friends and I changed schools, but it was an adventure.

3 Rachel: I felt wonderful on the first day. I was only fifteen but I had a job and some money. I didn't work on schooldays – only on Saturdays. And I sometimes worked in the holidays. Of course, the job was actually quite boring. Did they pay me much money? No, but I loved it – I really did.

4 Becky: They taught me at school and I took the test when I was sixteen. Then my mother lent me her car twice a week. Was I frightened? Well, the first time I drove alone I was frightened for about five minutes, but then I felt fine.

5 Marco: I love my parents but I was very happy to be free. When I left the house with all my suitcases, I thought, 'I'm an adult!' I went to the airport and caught a plane to Britain. I didn't know then that I would stay here for so long.

Focus

- Describing experiences
- Expressing feelings
- Past simple, all forms (regular and irregular verbs, *was/were, could*)

2 Read the descriptions in Exercise 1 again. Say which were good experiences for the speaker and which were bad experiences. Use adjectives from the texts to describe the speakers' feelings.

starting school *(bad)*
When Rosie started school, she was unhappy. She felt awful.

1 moving house
2 getting a job
3 driving
4 leaving home

DISCOVERING LANGUAGE

3 Work with your partner. Look again at the experiences described in Exercise 1.

1 Find the past simple form of these verbs. Make lists of regular and irregular verbs.

hate   be   take   cry   leave   feel   move   lose   change   have   work   love   teach   lend   drive   think   go   catch

REGULAR: *hate – hated ...*
IRREGULAR: *be – was ...*

2 Make rules for forming past simple questions and negative statements.

3 Some verbs form questions and negative statements in a different way. What are the rules for the past tense of the verb *to be*?

4 Work with a partner. Think of a time in your childhood when you did something new.
1. Ask your partner about his/her experience. Here are some questions to help you.
   What did you do that was new?   How old were you?
   How did you feel?
2. Write a paragraph about your own or your partner's experience.

5 Read the article below. Then ask and answer questions about Nicholas.

Where/computer lessons?
Where does Nicholas have computer lessons?

1. When/start/speak well?
2. When/begin/learn French?
3. When/learn/read?
4. Why/leave school?
5. What instrument/play?

DISCOVERING LANGUAGE

6 Find the past tense forms of *can* and *can't* in the article.

7 Now complete these sentences.

Nicholas ..... well before he was one.
Nicholas could speak well before he was one.

1. He ..... telephone messages at 18 months.
2. He ..... before he learnt to speak.
3. He corrected his father's spelling when he ..... .
4. He ..... at school, because he was bored.
5. His teachers ..... special lessons.

8 Ask and answer. Find out what your partner could do as a child.

speak in sentences
A: *When could you speak in sentences?*
B: *I could speak in sentences when/before I was two.*

1. walk without help
2. read
3. write your name
4. ride a bicycle
5. understand a foreign language
6. use a computer

9 Write sentences about yourself as a child. Say what you could and could not do at certain ages.

THE FOUR-YEAR-OLD
COLLEGE STUDENT

A CHILD OF FOUR is studying at college because he is too intelligent for school. Nicholas MacMahon has computer lessons at the West London Institute.

Nicholas spoke well before he was one. At eighteen months he took telephone messages for his parents. At two he began to learn French. The strange thing about Nicholas is that he taught himself to read before he could speak.

'We knew immediately that he could read. When he could speak, he corrected my spelling,' said his father. When Nicholas went to school, his teachers gave him pictures to colour and toys to play with. He tried two different schools, but he was bored and unhappy and his parents decided that he couldn't stay there. His teachers did not have time to prepare special lessons for Nicholas. The MacMahons had no idea what to do with him. Then the West London Institute offered to help. Nicholas spends some of his time there, and also studies at home. Now he identifies insects by their Latin names. He reads the newspaper every day, and he can play the violin well. 'We don't have any social life,' Mr MacMahon said. 'Nicholas is our life. He is a clever child and we want to help him in every way.' ■

ENGLISH AROUND YOU

Go on! You can do it!

Development

READING

1 Look at the picture. Say what you think is happening. Then read the text and see if you were right.

As well as academic subjects to improve students' minds and prepare them for college, a lot of high schools in the United States offer vocational courses. These prepare students for particular jobs. At different high schools in California, students can learn how to become cooks and waiters in hotels and restaurants or mechanics and salespeople in garages and service stations. They can also train to be secretaries and receptionists.

The courses are available to high school students during the day as part of their normal school programme. In the evenings they are also available to other people who are not at the school.

Gene Abbott runs a course in automotive repair at San Rafael High School. He teaches his students how to repair cars. He gives some lessons in a classroom, but most of the course takes place in the workshop. It is a practical course, so students learn by doing as well as by studying.

Students begin by examining an engine in detail. They learn

2 What do these phrases mean? Find the phrases and explanations of them in the text.

1 academic subjects
2 vocational courses
3 a course in automotive repair
4 a practical course

3 Look at the pictures below. What jobs do these people do? Label them with words from the text.

secretary

4 Answer the questions.
1 What does Gene Abbott teach?
2 Who can attend the vocational courses at the school:
   a) in the day?
   b) in the evening?

LISTENING

5 🔊 Listen to Gene Abbott and answer the questions.
1 How old are his students?
2 What percentage (%) of his students are girls?
3 How many hours a week do the students spend with him?
4 How much does the course cost?
5 Why do students take this course?
6 How many lessons a week are in the classroom?
7 Does the student, Josh Lofrano, like the course? Why (not)?

SPEAKING

6 Discuss vocational courses for schoolchildren in your country. List the skills that these courses teach and the jobs that they prepare students for.

WRITING

7 Read this letter. The writer is asking for more information about a course.
1 Put these in the order they appear in the letter:
   a) the address that Steven is writing to
   b) the date
   c) Steven's address
2 Which paragraph:
   a) says when Steven can do a course?
   b) gives his reason for writing?
   c) asks for details?
3 Why does Steven end *Yours faithfully*?

291B Fourth Street
San Rafael
California
May 2nd

Careers Guidance Center
Las Galinas Avenue
San Rafael
California CA94913

Dear Sir/Madam

1– I am writing to ask for information about courses in automotive repair. I enjoy working with cars and would like to train to be a mechanic.

2– I would like to start a course in September but I can only study in the evenings because I have a full-time day job.

3– Please send me details and an application form.

Yours faithfully,

Steven Ackerman

---

8 Now write a similar letter about any course that interests you. You can start a course in April, but you are only free in the afternoons. Use your real address and today's date.

Summary

FUNCTIONAL LANGUAGE

Talking about intentions
I'm going to learn Japanese.

Talking about ability
How well can you speak French?
Very well./Well./A little./Not at all.
I can speak it very well./I can't speak it at all.

Saying what you like
I like/enjoy painting.

GRAMMAR

Past simple (revision)
AFFIRMATIVE: I learnt Spanish.
NEGATIVE: I didn't learn Greek.
INTERROGATIVE: Did you learn Arabic?

Past simple verb *to be* (revision)
AFFIRMATIVE: I/he/she/it was there.
You/we/they were there.
NEGATIVE: I/he/she/it wasn't here.
You/we/they weren't here.
INTERROGATIVE: Was I/he/she/it good?
Were you/we/they good?

Verb structures
want/would like + *to* + infinitive

Adverbs of degree
very well, well, a little, not at all

Modal: *could*
AFFIRMATIVE: He *could* read well.
NEGATIVE: I *couldn't* swim.
INTERROGATIVE: *Could* they help?

***Going to* + infinitive**
I am
you are
he/she/it is   (not) going to + infinitive
we are
they are

INTERROGATIVE AND SHORT ANSWERS
Are you going to leave soon?
Yes, I am./No, I'm not.

See the Grammar Reference section at the back of the book for more information.

3 Planning a trip

Ways of travelling

Focus

- Means of transport
- Making comparisons
- Comparative adjectives (+ *er* and *more*)
- Comparative adjectives (irregular forms)
- Prefer + ing

1 Look at the different types of transport above. Match the pictures with the words below.

boat   car   helicopter   balloon   bicycle (bike)   bus   coach   plane   ship

2 Work with a partner. Group the words in Exercise 1 in the categories below. Use a dictionary to help you.
1 private: *car*   public: …
1 private and public transport
2 vehicles that you use for short distances and long distances
3 vehicles that you drive, ride, sail and fly
4 vehicles that a pilot, driver, and rider controls

3 Say which kind of transport you usually use.

During the week, I usually travel around town by bus. At weekends I often drive to friends' houses or into the country. When I go on holiday, I travel by train.

4 Look at the title of the magazine article. What do you think the writer's main points are? Now read the article. Were you right? Do you agree with her?

FEAR OF FLYING

How can anyone like flying? It's a crazy thing to do. Birds fly; people don't. I hate flying. You wait for hours for the plane to take off, and it's often late. The plane's always crowded. You can't walk around and there's nothing to do. You can't open the windows and you can't get off. The seats are uncomfortable, there's no choice of food and there are never enough toilets. Then after the plane lands, it's even worse. It takes hours to get out of the airport and into the city.

I prefer travelling by train. Trains are much better than planes; they're cheaper, safer, and more comfortable. You can walk around in a train and open the windows. Stations are more convenient than airports, because you can get on and off in the middle of cities. If you miss a train, you can always catch another one later. Yes, trains are slower, but speed isn't everything. Staying alive and enjoying yourself is more important!

5 Read the article again and answer these questions.
1 How does the writer prefer travelling?
2 For the writer, which of these adjectives describe travelling by train? Which adjectives describe travelling by plane?

dangerous   fast   safe   bad   slow
expensive   comfortable   good
uncomfortable   convenient

6 Now match these verbs from the text and their definitions.

1 to land
2 to catch
3 to miss
4 to take off

a) to leave the ground and go up in the air
b) to arrive at an airport in a plane
c) to arrive too late for a plane, train, etc.
d) to get on or into public transport

DISCOVERING LANGUAGE

7 Look back at the article and answer the questions.
1 What is the comparative form of these adjectives?
safe – *safer*
safe   comfortable   convenient   cheap
slow   important   good   bad
2 What rules can you make about the comparative form of:
a) most short adjectives?
b) long adjectives?
Are there any irregular adjectives that do not fit these rules?
3 Complete this sentence with the word used to compare two things:
Stations are more convenient ..... airports.

8 🎧 Stress and intonation. Listen. Mark the main stresses in these sentences. Then listen again and underline the /ə/ sounds.
1 Trains are safer than planes.
2 Stations are more convenient than airports.

Practise saying these sentences. Then write three sentences comparing two things in your classroom and read them to your partner.

9 🎧 Listen to five people and say how they prefer travelling and why. Complete the chart.

	HOW?	WHY?
Alan	*plane*	*faster*
Anna	.....	.....
Becky	.....	.....
Sally	.....	.....
Bob	.....	.....

10 Now write about Bob.
He prefers travelling ... because ...

🔄 COMPARING CULTURES

11 Write about common ways of travelling short and long distances in your country. Compare the different ways and say which you prefer. Use these adjectives to help you.

slow/fast   cheap/expensive
safe/dangerous   comfortable/uncomfortable
convenient/inconvenient   reliable/unreliable

Travel arrangements

Focus

- Travel

- Talking about intentions for the future
- Making decisions
- Inviting someone
- Making promises

- Modal: *will* for future decisions
- *I'll* + infinitive for promises
- *Let's* + infinitive
- Further practice: *going to* for intentions, *would you like* + infinitive with *to*

1 🔊 **Listen and read. Julia Marsh is talking to a colleague. His name is James Brady. Answer the questions.**

1 Who is going to visit Edinburgh?
2 Who is going to visit Glasgow?
3 What is the reason for their trips?

JULIA: James, have you got a meeting in Edinburgh soon?
JAMES: Yes, I'm going to see some clients on the 20th. Why?
JULIA: Oh, because I'm going to visit clients in Glasgow on Wednesday, and it's quite near Edinburgh.
JAMES: Ah ... I'm going to drive there on the Friday before, but that's no good to you. How will you get there?
JULIA: I'll go by car too, I think. No, I won't drive – it's a long way. I'll fly. Then I can go and come back the same day.
JAMES: Good idea. I need my car because I want to do some sightseeing.

2 Look at the calendar. Say when:

1 James is going to meet his clients.
2 Julia is going to meet her clients.
3 James is going to travel to Scotland.
4 Julia is going to travel to Scotland.

DISCOVERING LANGUAGE

3 Look at the conversation again and answer the questions.

1 There are two main verb structures in the conversation which refer to the future. What are they?
2 Find three sentences in which the speaker is making a decision about the future during the conversation. Which verb structure is used?
3 Find three sentences where the speaker is referring to an intention. Which verb structure is used?

4 Four friends are going to go camping. Before they go, they need to do the things on the list below. Work in pairs.

Student A: Look at the list. Ask questions to find out who is going to do which task.
Student B: Turn to page 117. Answer your partner's questions.

A: Who's going to ... ?
B: Paula is.
A: Is Paula going to ... ?
B: Yes, she is./No, she isn't.

People: Paula, John, Penny, Tim

Things to do:
borrow the tent
get passports
buy the plane tickets
change some money
buy the sleeping bags
find the guidebook

5 There are some last-minute tasks to do before Paula and her friends leave, but they haven't got time to do everything. What does each person say?

JOHN AND PENNY:
– clean the bath ✗ / make some coffee ✓
We won't clean the bath now.
We'll make some coffee.
– sweep the floor ✗ / have breakfast ✓
– wash the dishes ✗ / shut the windows ✓

TIM:
– make the bed ✗ / pack my bag ✓

PAULA:
– phone my mother ✗ / phone for a taxi ✓

6 Listen and read. Marco is talking to his friend Teresa. As you read, find:
a) an invitation d) an intention
b) a suggestion   e) a decision
c) a promise

MARCO: I'm going to *Brighton* at the weekend. Would you like to come?
TERESA: Oh, yes. I'd love to.
MARCO: Oh, good. I'm going to catch the *ten o'clock train*. Is that OK?
TERESA: That's fine.
MARCO: Don't be late. It's the only *fast train*.
TERESA: Don't worry. I'll be there.
MARCO: Let's meet at *the ticket office* at *half past nine*. Or earlier at your flat?
TERESA: Er ... no, I'll see you at *the ticket office*.

7 Practise reading the conversation with your partner.

8 Work in pairs. Practise similar conversations.
Student A: You are Marco. Use the information below to replace the phrases in italics in Exercise 6.

> You are going to Oxford on Saturday. The direct coach leaves at 11.30. Arrange to meet at the coach stop 15 minutes before.

Student B: You are Teresa. Turn to page 117.
Now change places.

9 Julia is asking Rita to make some travel arrangements. Listen to their conversation, look at Rita's notes and correct her mistakes.

> Book plane ticket for Julia.
>
> London–Glasgow, Wednesday 15th, 2 p.m. First class, non-smoking.

10 Rita is looking at a train timetable. Use the correct form of her notes and say which train she books.

11 Now answer the questions about Julia's train.
1 What time does it leave London?
2 Which station does it leave from?
3 What time does it arrive in Glasgow?
4 How many times does it stop before it arrives there?
5 Is there food and drink on the train?

ENGLISH AROUND YOU

Development

SPEAKING

1 Look at this picture of Sherry McGonegle. What do you think her job is?

2 Match the descriptions to the pictures, and then say which of the tasks you think she does.

Picture 1   *search bags*
issue tickets   search bags   change money
check in luggage   re-confirm flights   give seat numbers

LISTENING

3 🔊 Listen to the first part of an interview with Sherry. She is talking about her job. Check your answers to Exercises 1 and 2.

4 🔊 Now listen to the second part and answer the questions.
1 What are the three classes of ticket that you can buy on this airline?
2 What does Sherry say about her job? Are these sentences true or false?
   a) It's boring.
   b) Her colleagues are nice.
   c) A lot of the passengers are unpleasant.

5 🔊 Listen to Sherry's conversations with three different passengers.

Conversation 1. Choose the best answers to complete these sentences.
1 The first passenger is going to
   a) carry his bag on to the plane.   b) check the bag in.
2 He's travelling to   a) Canada.   b) California.   c) Ohio.

Conversation 2. Complete the information.
3 Flight number from Chicago: .....   5 Arrival gate in Chicago: .....
4 Departure gate: .....

Conversation 3. Complete the information.
6 Day of departure from Vancouver: .....   8 Arrival time: .....
7 Departure time: .....

TRAIN versus PLANE

A race against TIME

THE FLIGHT TIME FROM London to Edinburgh is just under an hour. On a good day, the train from King's Cross to Waverley takes four hours. End of story? No, not quite. This story begins in Trafalgar Square, central London, at 7.30 a.m. It ends in the same place 8 hours 30 minutes later.

READING

6 Read the article and complete the chart.

LONDON – EDINBURGH	
Means of transport	*taxi*, ...
Total time	.....
Total cost	.....
EDINBURGH – LONDON	
Means of transport	*taxi*, ...
Total time	.....
Total cost	.....

BY PLANE

The first stop is Heathrow Airport by taxi for the nine o'clock plane. The traffic is not bad and we reach Heathrow in forty-five minutes. We complete check-in and security checks by 8.30 a.m. A loudspeaker announces a delay of ten minutes. It is time for coffee. But at 9.14 our Boeing 757 is leaving the gate. At 9.27 we are in the air, and stewardesses are trying to serve a quick, free breakfast to a full plane. The plane lands at 10.20, and ten minutes later we are in the airport terminal. There is a coach outside, and we reach the centre of Edinburgh in half an hour. It is a short walk to the Scott Monument in Princes Street. It is 11.15.

BY TRAIN

We leave the monument and walk around the corner to Waverley Station to catch the Royal Scot. Our first class carriage is nearly empty. The train leaves Platform 19 at exactly 11.30 and hurries south through beautiful countryside. Lunch is excellent, but it costs a lot. We reach King's Cross two minutes early at 3.48 and take a taxi to Trafalgar Square, arriving at six minutes past four.

A standard British Airways single ticket to Edinburgh is £106. The taxi to Heathrow is £30, and the coach fare to Edinburgh city centre is £2.80. A single first class train ticket is £87. A taxi from King's Cross to Trafalgar Square is £6.70.

7 Now answer the questions.
1. Where exactly did each journey begin?
2. Name:
   a) a station in London.
   b) a station in Edinburgh.
   c) a London airport.
3. Are these sentences true or false?
   a) The plane was punctual.
   b) Breakfast was expensive.
   c) The plane was full.
   d) The train was punctual.
   e) Lunch was expensive.
   f) The first class carriage was full.

WRITING

8 You want to travel from London to Edinburgh. Consider the information above and decide if you will travel by plane or by first class train. Write a paragraph. Say what you will do and give reasons.

Summary

FUNCTIONAL LANGUAGE

Comparing things
Planes are faster than trains.
Travelling by train is more interesting than flying.

Making quick decisions
I'll buy the tickets.
We'll find a hotel.

Inviting someone
Would you like to come to Brighton?

Making suggestions
Let's meet at the ticket office.

Talking about preferences
I prefer travelling by train.

GRAMMAR

Comparative adjectives
REGULAR: SHORT ADJECTIVES
adjective + *(e)r*: *nicer, cheaper*
REGULAR: LONG ADJECTIVES
more + adjective: *more interesting*
IRREGULAR
good – better   bad – worse

***Will* for decisions**
AFFIRMATIVE
I/we   will/shall   + infinitive
I'll/we'll
NEGATIVE
I/we will not/shall not   + infinitive
I/we won't/shan't
INTERROGATIVE
Shall I/we + infinitive?

Making promises
I'll be there at 9.00.

Verb structure
prefer + -ing

See the Grammar Reference section at the back of the book for more information.

UNITS 1–3
Progress check 1

Vocabulary

1 Label each picture with a verb.

1 – walk

2 Match each verb with a noun that can follow it.

have – *a meal*

1 miss   a) a club
2 play   b) a boat
3 ride   c) a bus
4 sail   d) a language
5 do   e) a bicycle
6 cost   f) an instrument
7 join   g) some homework
8 speak   h) money

3 Name the official language.

China – *Chinese*

1 Japan   3 Portugal   5 Egypt
2 Germany   4 Argentina   6 Bangladesh

4 Write the names of the jobs.

He types letters and documents.
A typist
1 She prepares meals in a restaurant.
2 He serves food to people in a restaurant.
3 She works at the front desk of a hotel.
4 He checks people's teeth.
5 She repairs cars.

5 Complete the sentences with these adjectives.

convenient   difficult   safe   uncomfortable
reliable   cheap

1 The train journey was very ..... . It only cost five pounds.
2 The bus stop is outside our house. That's very ..... .
3 We sat on hard seats for three hours. The journey was very ..... .
4 I've got two small children and a dog, so it's ..... to use public transport.
5 Bye! Have a ..... journey, and call me when you get home!
6 We don't have any problems with our car. It's very ..... .

6 Write adjectives that mean the opposite of the ones in Exercise 5.

convenient – *inconvenient*

7 Look at the word box. Find nine more forms of transport.

z	o	s	h	i	p	b	f	i	p
c	d	b	u	r	a	l	s	e	l
o	g	y	k	l	c	t	a	x	i
a	t	x	l	u	a	e	h	n	j
c	p	o	t	k	r	b	l	d	e
h	o	c	r	q	i	u	w	m	a
n	b	o	a	t	v	s	i	e	d
h	e	l	i	c	o	p	t	e	r
y	f	a	n	k	e	l	p	r	o

Grammar and functions

8 Underline the correct form of each verb in the sentences below.

I *don't understand*/am not understanding.
1. They usually *visit/are visiting* their parents on Sundays.
2. My brother *travels/is travelling* in Thailand at the moment.
3. I *start/am starting* work at eight every morning and *finish/am finishing* at about four.
4. He *likes/is liking* old books.
5. Oh, John, hurry up! Clare *waits/is waiting* for you at the station.

9 Read the answers and complete the questions.

'..... on Sundays?'
'I go sailing.'
'What do you do on Sundays?'
1. '..... in restaurants?'
   'My parents? About once a week.'
2. '..... in July?'
   'We're going to travel around Italy.'
3. '..... her first computer?'
   'When she was twelve, I think.'
4. '..... Portuguese?'
   'Jim? Oh, quite well now.'
5. '..... to discos?'
   'Because she likes dancing and making new friends.'

10 Complete the sentences with the correct form of the verb in brackets.

I really like ..... (make) cakes.
I really like making cakes.
1. What do you enjoy ..... (do) in the evenings?
2. What would you like ..... (do) after school?
3. She wants ..... (buy) my cassette recorder.
4. I don't like tennis. I prefer ..... (swim).
5. Wait! I'll ..... (come) with you.

11 Complete the sentences with a negative form of the verb in brackets.

You ..... (be) at school yesterday.
You weren't at school yesterday.
1. I ..... (work) today.
2. She ..... (study) on Sundays.
3. They ..... (play) tennis tomorrow.
4. We ..... (go) on holiday last year.
5. I ..... (can hear) you.

12 Write the comparative form of these adjectives.

safe – *safer*
important – *more important*
1. comfortable   5 expensive
2. slow   6 bad
3. good   7 convenient
4. cheap   8 old

13 Complete the conversation. Paula is phoning a friend.

PAULA: Hi, Jane. How are you?
JANE: Fine, thanks. What about you?
PAULA: Oh, I'm OK. Listen, I've got two tickets for the theatre tonight, to see *Cats*. Would (1) ..... ?
JANE: Well, I've got a lot of work, but yes, I (2) ..... . What time does it start?
PAULA: At half past seven, but (3) ..... at seven.
JANE: OK. Where? In front of the theatre?
PAULA: Yes, OK. Are you sure you can come?
JANE: Don't worry. I (4) ..... there!

Common errors

14 Add one word to correct each sentence.

We like bungee jumping because is exciting.
We like bungee jumping because it is exciting.
1. I meet you at the station at five.
2. I'm going to go evening classes.
3. How you say 'agua' in English?
4. He visits his parents three four times a year.
5. She can speak Arabic at all.

15 Correct the word order.

It's a hobby very relaxing.
It's a very relaxing hobby.
1. We play twice a week basketball.
2. I can write very well English.
3. They together do the housework.
4. She's going next week to paint her flat.
5. We will a flight to Berlin book.

> At the end of the Progress Check, look back at your mistakes and study the Grammar Reference section for further help.

4 Shopping for clothes

Describing clothes

Focus

- Clothes
- Describing clothes
- Asking about problems
- Saying what is wrong
- Adjectives and order of adjectives
- *Too* + adjective
- *Not* + adjective + *enough*
- Further practice: present tenses

blouse shoes sweater
cardigan T-shirt tie
earrings dress shirt
jeans trousers
gloves waistcoat
boots coat
sweatshirt

tights belt
socks scarf
sandals hat
jacket
trainers

1 Work in pairs. Look at the people in the picture and match the clothes they are wearing with the labels.

2 🔊 Listen to the people in the picture above describing their clothes. Name each person in the picture.
Jo   Winston   Mark   Emma   Stephanie

3 Describe the clothes of another person in the class. Can other students guess who you are describing?
She's wearing a shirt, jeans and a jacket.

4 Choose a picture of a person from any unit in this book. Write a description of the person's clothes. Use the rule in the chart about the order of adjectives, and the adjectives below, to help you.

(ARTICLE)	ADJECTIVES		NOUN
	QUALITY	COLOUR	
(a)	long beautiful	blue brown	jacket shoes

big/small   long/short   tight/loose   cheap/expensive   attractive/ugly
She's wearing a long black dress and a beautiful red jacket.

5 Look at the picture below. Say where Julia is and what she is doing.

6 🔊 There are problems with each coat that Julia tries on. Listen and match the problems, a)–c), with each of the coats.
a) (length) It isn't long enough.
b) (colour) She doesn't like the colour.
c) (size) It's too small.

32

DISCOVERING LANGUAGE

7 Look again at the sentences in Exercise 6.
1 Make rules about the position of the words *too* and *enough*.
2 Now look at the pictures below and describe the problems with the clothes in two ways. Ask and answer:
A: *What's wrong with the sweater?*
B: *It's too small./It's not big enough.*

8 Look at the clothes in Exercise 1. Say which you would/would not like to buy and why. Use some of the adjectives below. Check their meaning in your dictionary.
trendy   old-fashioned   dark
bright   dull   baggy
I wouldn't buy the gloves. They're too bright.

9 Stress and intonation. Listen and repeat.
1 I like this coat, not that one.
2 The red one is cheaper than the green one.

Underline the contrasting words in these sentences. Then listen and check.
3 These shoes are too big, and those are too small.
4 It's a nice dress, but it's too expensive.
5 I want a coat, not a jacket.
6 I like the black jeans. The blue ones aren't long enough.

10 Read about Jean Douglas and her husband Patrick. Answer the questions.
1 How does Jean decide to dress:
   a) at work?
   b) at other times?
2 Who chooses Patrick's clothes?
3 How does Patrick dress when he visits his parents?
4 What about you? Do you dress for yourself or for other people?

Who do you dress for?

When I was young, my mother chose my clothes. Now I dress for myself, but I also want to look attractive to other people – especially my husband. I don't wear certain colours like black and yellow because they don't suit me and Patrick doesn't like them. At work, of course, I have no choice – I'm a tour guide, so I have to wear the company uniform. At home I usually wear casual clothes.

I dress for the weather! No, that's not true. I want to look nice, but I hate shopping. Jean buys a lot of my clothes and I like them. They're fashionable but practical. When I visit my parents, I dress for them. They don't like jeans and T-shirts, so I wear smarter clothes.

11 Work with your partner. Ask and answer. Then tell the class about your partner.
Who chooses your clothes?
Which colours suit you?
Which colours don't suit you?
Do you like tight or loose clothes?
Do you like smart or casual clothes?

The right clothes

1 Look at the picture of the shop window. Say what clothes this shop sells.

It sells shoes, ...

2 Match the labels with the T-shirts.

Focus

- Clothes sizes
- Countries
- Saying what size clothes someone takes
- Buying clothes
- Superlative adjectives (*-est, most* and irregular forms)
- Further practice: comparative adjectives (irregular forms)

3 Work with your partner. Ask and answer.

A: *What size T-shirt do you take?*
B: *(Medium).*

4 Look at the chart of European and British clothes sizes. Ask and answer about the sizes that Marco and Teresa need in Britain.

A: *What size shirt does Marco take?*
B: *He takes size fifteen and a half.*
MARCO   Shirt: 40   Jacket: 52   Shoes: 42
TERESA   Blouse: 38   Dress: 38   Shoes: 39

WOMEN					
Dresses, suits and blouses					
Europe	38	40	42	44	46
UK	10	12	14	16	18
Shoes					
Europe	37	38	39	40	41
UK	4½	5½	6	6½	7½

MEN					
Suits and jackets					
Europe	46	48	50	52	54
UK	36	38	40	42	44
Shirts					
Europe	39	41	43	45	
UK	15	16	17	18	
Shoes					
Europe	41	42	43	44	45
UK	7	8	8½-9	9½-10	11

5 🔊 Listen and read. Marco is in the shop.

MARCO: I'd like a *pair of black shoes*, please.
ASSISTANT: Certainly. What size?
MARCO: Um ... *eight*, I think.
ASSISTANT: Here you are. Would you like to try them on?
MARCO: Yes, please ... I'm afraid they're too *small*. Can I try *eight and a half*, please.
ASSISTANT: Certainly. Here you are.
MARCO: Thanks ... They're fine. I'll take them. Oh, how much are they?
ASSISTANT: They're *£24.99*.

6 Work in pairs. Practise similar conversations.

Student A: You are the customer. Buy different clothes. When you speak, change the words in italics and the pronouns.
Student B: Turn to page 117. You are the assistant.

UNIT FOUR

7 🔊 Listen. Marco is in another clothes shop. Describe the jacket that he buys.

DISCOVERING LANGUAGE

8 Complete the comparative column of the chart. Then listen again to Marco.

ADJECTIVE	COMPARATIVE	SUPERLATIVE
nice	.....	.....
cheap	.....	(the) cheapest
expensive	.....	.....
beautiful	.....	(the) most beautiful
good	.....	.....
bad	.....	(the) worst

1 Complete the third column with superlative forms.
2 Say which adjectives have irregular comparative and superlative forms.
3 Make a rule about the two sorts of regular superlative forms. When do we use *most*?

9 Complete the sentences with the superlative form of each adjective.
1 I think Clint Eastwood is the (attractive) American actor.
2 My (good) friend is my sister.
3 My (bad) mistake was leaving home at 17.
4 The (difficult) thing about English is choosing the right preposition.
5 My (long) journey was from Mexico City to Miami by bus.

10 Change the sentences in Exercise 9 so that they are true for you. Then discuss your sentences with a partner.

11 Now write sentences using the superlative form of these adjectives.

long   dangerous   old   beautiful   good
expensive   high   bad

The River Loire is the longest river in France.
I think bungee jumping is the most dangerous sport of all.

🔄 COMPARING CULTURES

12 Look at these pictures of clothes from around the world and match the clothes to one of the countries.

Scotland   Japan   Peru   India
Morocco   Indonesia

I think the kilt is from Scotland.

Say if people wear any of these clothes in your country.

kilt | kimono | sari | sarong | poncho

13 Write about what you wear at different times of the year.

In my country it is very cold in winter. I usually wear a sweater, thick trousers and boots. When I go out I put on a warm coat. In summer it is very hot and most young people wear shorts and T-shirts. To go to work I wear cotton trousers and shirts with short sleeves.

Development

SPEAKING

1 Identify the jobs of the people in the picture below. Give reasons.

I think 1 is a student. Her clothes are very casual and comfortable ...

LISTENING

2 🔊 Now listen to a British person doing Exercise 1. What are the differences between her stereotypes and yours?

READING

3 Look at the photograph in the article and say what kind of work you think Niki does. Then look at the words below from the article and, without reading it, guess what the article says. Then read to see if you were right.

model   money   youngest   millionaire   pizza   company   high school   expensive restaurants

4 Are these statements true or false? Correct the false statements.
1 Niki leads the life of a normal American schoolgirl.
2 She is richer than her teachers.
3 She is only fourteen years old.
4 She has a good job as a model.
5 School is very important to her.
6 She enjoys eating in the most expensive restaurants all the time.

5 Find a word in the article that can mean the same as:
1 normal
2 a child who goes to school
3 an agreement in writing
4 the outside of a book or magazine
5 a school-leaving certificate
6 cream, etc. to add colour to your face

WRITING

6 Do you have strong feelings about the clothes you wear? Do you feel good when you wear some clothes and bad when you wear others?

Read the extract on the right from a letter and then write a paragraph about an item of clothing that is important to you.

Niki inc.

Niki Taylor is an average healthy all-American schoolkid – except that she is director of her own company and can earn more money in a day than her teachers earn in a year.

At the age of fourteen Niki signed a two-year contract with L'Oreal, the cosmetics company, and at sixteen she became the youngest model ever to appear on the cover of the fashion magazine Vogue. Today, at seventeen, she is a multi-millionaire and has her own company, Niki Inc., to manage her business activities as one of the world's most popular models. But she wants to stay at high school for a little longer. 'I want to get my high school diploma so I can go to college when the modelling finishes. Then I can start a different kind of business.'

She is already finding it difficult to continue a normal life at home and school because her success is too well-known. Everyone expects her to wear beautiful clothes and make-up all the time and to eat in expensive restaurants. Sometimes all she wants to do is put on an old pair of jeans and go and eat pizza with her girlfriends. 'I want to be myself, and not always 'Niki Taylor – The Model'.'

I think the nicest – and the oldest – thing I have is this black jacket. I feel good when I wear it. It's loose and comfortable, and it suits me. I can wear it with anything; it's smart when I wear it with a dress, and casual when I wear it with jeans. It wasn't expensive. I bought it in a second-hand shop three years ago, and it only cost two pounds!

UNIT FOUR

Summary

FUNCTIONAL LANGUAGE

Asking about problems
What's wrong with the sweater?
It's too small. / It's not long enough.

Asking about clothes sizes
What size T-shirt do you take?
Medium. / Size 12.

Asking to try clothes
Can I try this on?

Agreeing to buy something
I'll take it.

GRAMMAR

Superlative adjectives
SHORT ADJECTIVES: REGULAR
cheap – (the) cheapest
thin – (the) thinnest
ugly – (the) ugliest
SHORT ADJECTIVES: IRREGULAR
good – (the) best
bad – (the) worst
LONG ADJECTIVES
expensive – (the) most expensive

Too / not … enough
too + adjective: *too short*
not + adjective + enough: *not long enough*

Order of adjectives (revision)

ADJECTIVES		NOUN
QUALITY	COLOUR	
short	blue	jacket

See the Grammar Reference section at the end of the book for more information.

5 The rules of the road

Problems with vehicles

Focus

- Traffic signs
- Parts of a motorbike

- Talking about what is possible or permitted
- Talking about rules and obligations
- Explaining a problem

- Have to/ don't have to + infinitive
- Further practice: can/ can't + infinitive

1 🔊 Rita is meeting a friend at a coach station. Listen to the first part of her conversation with a traffic warden and answer the questions.

1 What's the problem?
2 What's the solution?

WARDEN: Excuse me.
RITA: Yes?
WARDEN: You can't park here.
RITA: But it's only for a few minutes. I'm waiting for a friend.
WARDEN: This is a taxi rank. You can park in the car park. It's just round the corner.

DISCOVERING LANGUAGE

2 Match sentences 1 and 2 with the explanations of the uses of *can('t)*.

1 You can't park here.
2 You can park in the car park.

a) There is a rule, so you have no choice.
b) It is a possibility, but it is your decision.

3 🔊 Listen and read. Answer the questions.

1 What time does Rita start work?
2 Is there a fee for using the car park?

RITA: But I have to be at work at nine o'clock.
WARDEN: The car park is very near here and you don't have to pay. Are you going to move or do you want a parking ticket?
RITA: No, no, I'll move. I'm going now. Sorry.

DISCOVERING LANGUAGE

4 Match sentences 1 and 2 with the explanations of the uses of *(don't) have to*.

1 I have to be at work at nine o'clock.
2 You don't have to pay.

a) There is no obligation.
b) There is an obligation or a rule.

5 Look at the pictures. Complete these sentences with *has to* or *doesn't have to*.

1 Car A ..... leave now.
2 It ..... stay here.
3 Car B ..... leave now.
4 It ..... stay here.

6 🔊 Pronunciation. Listen. Which sound can you hear?
1 /f/ or /v/? have to   2 /s/ or /z/? has to

7 Work in pairs. One of you is the traffic warden. One of you is Rita. Close your books and act out their conversation.

🗘 COMPARING CULTURES

8 In many countries mopeds are more popular than they are in the UK. Work in pairs.

Student A: Look at the chart. Ask your partner about the laws for riding mopeds in the UK and complete the column. Then complete the last column about your country.
Student B: Turn to page 118. Answer your partner's questions.

	UK	YOUR COUNTRY
wear a crash helmet?	Yes	.....
have a driving licence?	.....	.....
be 16 years old?	.....	.....
ride on motorways?	.....	.....
ride on cycle paths?	.....	.....
carry more than one person on the back?	.....	.....

A: *Do moped riders have to wear crash helmets in the UK?*
B: *Yes, they do.*
A: *Can they ride on motorways?*

9 Look at the picture of Alan's motorbike and label the parts. Use a dictionary to help you.

wheel   tyre   seat   handlebars   engine   petrol tank   brakes   lights   indicators

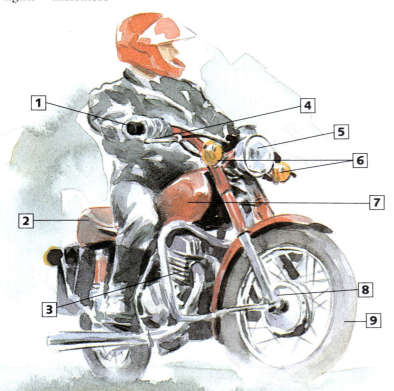

10 🔊 Listen. Alan is at a garage. What's wrong with his motorbike?

11 Work in pairs.
Student A: You are a customer. Take the things in the pictures back to your partner's shop.
Student B: You are a shop assistant. Ask about the problem. Suggest a solution.

A: Excuse me. There's something wrong with ...
B: Oh? What's the matter with it/them?
A: ...
B: ...

It's not working.

It's broken!   It's got a mark on it.

It's got a hole in it.

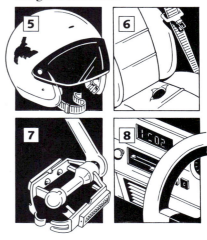

Focus

- Roads and driving
- *Had to/didn't have to* + infinitive
- Further practice: past simple

On the road

1 Look at the four pictures above. Describe what you think is happening in each one.

2 Read these headlines. What do you think the articles are about?
1 WRONG COLOUR?
2 FAST LANE DRAMA
3 WHERE'S MY BABY?!
4 L-DRIVER SAVES INSTRUCTOR

Now read the articles quickly and match them to the headlines and the pictures.

1
Learner driver Jeff Metcalfe saved the life of his instructor by driving him to hospital after only ninety minutes' driving experience.

When instructor Richard Brownhill had a heart attack in the passenger seat, Jeff had to drive through five miles of city centre traffic.

'There was a lot of traffic, so I didn't have to drive fast,' Jeff said yesterday. 'I just had to keep calm and try to remember my first lesson.' Doctors are now telling Richard to find a more relaxing job. But first he's going to finish Jeff's lessons – free.

2
Last week a seventy-eight year old pensioner drove the wrong way down the fast lane of a motorway at 30 kph.

Helmut Braun drove past the exit for Baden-Baden on the A5. He realised his mistake twenty kilometres later, did a U-turn and drove the wrong way down the fast lane. Another driver contacted the police, and a police car led him off the motorway.

Helmut had to pay a 1,000 DM fine. He can't drive for twelve months and after that he has to take another driving test.

3
Julie Harris of Flimwell, Sussex had eleven accidents in her Mini Metro last year. The last one happened a week ago when she was at some traffic lights and someone crashed into the back of her car. Yesterday she painted the car yellow after reading that yellow cars have fewer accidents. ●

4
JOAN PENDLETON from Boston, USA, was amazed to see her neighbours drive away with a baby's carrycot on the roof of their car – with their new baby still in it.

'We were in a hurry. Ken put the baby on the car roof because he had to open the car door. Then we drove away,' said the baby's mother, Sandy Bryson.

'We went about a hundred yards down the road and then I turned round to check the baby. That's when I found that he wasn't there. I screamed at my husband, "Ken, where's Tommy?" and he stopped the car.'

Fortunately, Tommy was fine. 'I don't know how it happened. We're so lucky that he wasn't hurt,' said Ken. ■

3 Work in pairs. Read the articles more carefully and then ask and answer the questions.

Student A: Read Articles 3 and 4. Then ask your partner these questions about Articles 1 and 2.

ARTICLE 1
1. What does 'L' mean in the headline?
2. Who are Richard and Jeff?
3. What happened to the instructor?
4. What did the pupil have to do? Why was this a problem?
5. How is the instructor going to thank his pupil?

ARTICLE 2
1. What did Helmut Braun do wrong?
2. How did this happen?
3. How much did he have to pay?
4. What can't he do for a year?
5. What does he have to do in a year's time?

Student B: Read Articles 1 and 2 and answer your partner's questions. Then ask these questions about Articles 3 and 4.

ARTICLE 3
1. What happened to Julie Harris last week?
2. What did she do yesterday?
3. Why did she do it?

ARTICLE 4
1. Who are these people: Tommy Bryson, Sandy Bryson, Ken Bryson, Joan Pendleton?
2. Where was the baby when a neighbour saw it? Why was it there?
3. What did the mother do when she saw that the baby wasn't in the car?
4. How was the baby?

4 Look at the articles again and find:
1. five examples of *regular* past simple verb forms.
2. the past simple forms of these *irregular* verbs:
   drive   do   lead   go   put   find

DISCOVERING LANGUAGE

5 Look at Article 1 again and find past simple affirmative and negative forms of the verb *have to*.

6 Now complete the sentences with the correct form (and tense) of *have to*.

..... he ..... leave yesterday?
Did he have to leave yesterday?

1. These days she often ..... work until six o'clock.
2. You ..... go if you don't want to.
3. I ..... move, but I liked the new flat.
4. ..... we ..... go home now?
5. They ..... catch a train because the plane was too expensive.

7 Match these words from the articles with their definitions.

1 – c
1. a pensioner   3. a fine   5. a yard
2. a lane   4. a roof   6. a carrycot

a) a part of a wide road for faster or slower vehicles
b) three feet or 0.914 metres
c) an older person who no longer works
d) the top cover of a vehicle or building
e) a baby's bed which you can carry
f) money that you have to pay when you do something wrong

8 Complete the sentences with the correct form of one of the verbs below.

contact   paint   have to   pay   save   take
happen   have   drive

Jeff Metcalfe ..... the life of his instructor.
Jeff Metcalfe saved the life of his instructor.

1. The instructor ..... a heart attack in the car.
2. Jeff ..... drive the car himself.
3. A pensioner ..... the wrong way along a motorway.
4. Did another driver ..... the police?
5. Did Helmut have to ..... a fine?
6. Does he have to ..... another driving test?
7. When did June's last accident ..... ?
8. She didn't ..... her car green; she ..... it yellow.

ENGLISH AROUND YOU

Development

SPEAKING

1 Look at the photographs.
1. What is the man's job?
2. Which side of the road do you drive on in your country? Which side do people drive on in Britain?
3. Which vehicles can't use motorways in your country?

READING

2 Read the article about Mark Hill's job and answer the questions below.
1. How many hours a day do Mark Hill and his colleagues usually work?
2. How many accidents are there in a normal 24-hour period?
3. After an accident, does Mark:
   a) close the motorway?
   b) help injured people?
   c) move accident vehicles off the road?
   d) interview other drivers?
4. Why do most accidents on motorways happen?

Mark Hill is a traffic police officer in Watford, near London. He works on some of the busiest motorways in Britain, the M1 and the M25.

'There are traffic police on duty twenty-four hours a day. There are three shifts, and each shift is eight hours. On average we have to deal with three to four accidents each shift.

'We deal with anyone in the accident who is injured. That's the first thing. Then we have to clear the road and get the traffic moving again.

'Most accidents happen because people drive too fast – especially when the roads are wet. Sometimes we get accidents that occur because drivers don't follow the rules. For example, I've seen a number of cases of drivers overtaking on the left. This is illegal in Britain. If you want to overtake, you have to go into the fast lane on the right.

'Not everyone can use a motorway in Britain. People that can't are pedal cyclists, motorcyclists on small motorbikes, people driving agricultural vehicles and, of course, pedestrians.

'I like my job. I have a varied working day – I never know what I'm going to do from one day to the next. And I meet all kinds of people. I don't think there's any other job that can give you that experience.'

3 Now complete the chart to show the use of motorways in Britain. Use information from the article above.

✓ can use motorways
✗ can't use motorways
? some of these can't use motorways

Cars	✓
Lorry drivers	
Pedal cyclists	
Motorcyclists	
Buses	
Agricultural vehicles	
Pedestrians	

4 What do the diagrams show about the law for overtaking in Britain?

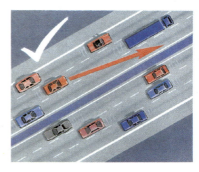

42

LISTENING

5 🔊 Listen to this radio announcement about traffic problems. Which picture shows what the radio announcer suggests?

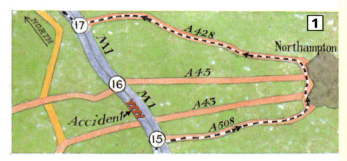

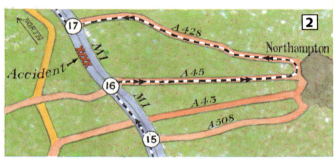

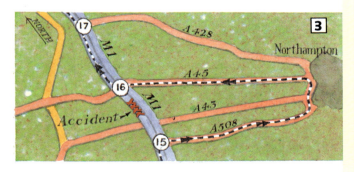

SPEAKING

6 Tell your partner about something that happened on the road. Perhaps it happened to you or you saw it or read about it. Answer your partner's questions about it.

WRITING

7 Write a short article about your partner's experience. Use these questions to help you.
What happened? (accident? crash?)
What did you see?
When and where did it happen?
What happened next?

UNIT FIVE

Summary

FUNCTIONAL LANGUAGE

Talking about rules and obligations
You (don't) have to be seventeen.
Do I have to wear a safety helmet?
You can't park here.

Talking about what is possible or permitted
You can park in the car park.
You can take one and a half hours for lunch.

Talking about problems
What's the matter (with it/them)?
What's wrong (with it/them)?
There's something wrong with my bike.
It's not working.
It's broken.
It's got a hole in it/a mark on it.

GRAMMAR

Modal *can/can't* for possibility/permission/prohibition
can/can't + infinitive

***have to* for obligation**
AFFIRMATIVE
I/you/we/they have to go.
He/she/it has to go.

NEGATIVE
I/you/we/they don't have to go.
He/she/it doesn't have to go.

INTERROGATIVE
Do I/you/we/they have to go?
Does he/she/it have to go?

SHORT ANSWERS
Yes, I/you/we/they do.
Yes, he/she/it does.
No, I/you/we/they don't.
No, he/she/it doesn't.

PAST SIMPLE FORMS
had to
did not/didn't have to

See the Grammar Reference section at the back of the book for more information.

43

6 How things work

Victorian inventions

Focus

- Inventions
- Talking about function
- Giving instructions
- Imperatives
- Sequence words: *first, then*
- *For + ing*

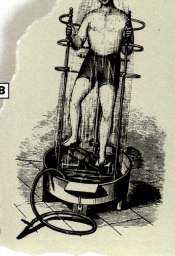

1 Look at the pictures of nineteenth-century inventions. Match the descriptions below with the pictures.

What is it? What's it for?
1 It's a special hat. It's for keeping the sun off your head.
2 It's a small electric train. It's for carrying food from the kitchen to the dining table.

DISCOVERING LANGUAGE

2 Study the sentences above. What form of the verb comes after the word *for*?
It's for . . . . .

3 Complete the sentences below with the correct form of the verb in brackets. Then match the sentences with the pictures.

It's for . . . . . (keep) your moustache dry.
It's for keeping your moustache dry.

1 It's for . . . . . (wash) yourself.
2 It's for . . . . . (print) advertisements on the street.
3 It's for . . . . . (serve) food.

4 🔊 Pronunciation. Listen and check your answers to Exercise 3. Then listen again and repeat. Notice the /ə/ sound in *for*.

🔊 Listen to these questions. How is *for* pronounced? Make a rule about different pronunciations of *for*.
What's it for? What's that for?

5 Say what each of the objects in the pictures below is for. Then write sentences.

1 *A bottle opener is for opening bottles.*

1 bottle opener   2 coffee maker   3 fax machine   4 camera

44

6 Look around the classroom. Ask and answer.
A: What's that bag for?
B: It's for carrying my books.

7 Read the instructions and say which invention they describe. Then identify the parts that the words in italics describe.

First, pull down the *lever* under the *shower-head*. This turns the water on. Don't get in until the water is the right temperature. Then climb in. Hold the *rails* with both hands and put your feet on the *pedals*. The pedals control the water from the shower-head. Press down with your right foot and then with your left. Don't press too hard. When you finish, climb out and push the lever up again. This turns the water off.

DISCOVERING LANGUAGE

8 Find verb forms in the text above that are used to give:
1 instructions   2 negative instructions
Explain how these verbs are formed.

9 Write instructions for the use of the invention in Picture A. Here are some verbs to help you:

stop   start   take   put   reach   send   move

10 Talk to your partner. Look at the inventions again. Do we use any of them today? Say why (not).

The tricycle printing press is not very practical today because the roads are busy. Also, I don't think you can write on the street. Other ways of advertising are cheaper and more effective.

11 Can you think of things which we use today that people invented over 100 years ago? Here are a few ideas. Add some more.

telephones   trains   cars   lifts

12 Think about how to use one of the inventions on your list. Make notes and then explain to your partner. Give instructions. Keep your notes for later.

Focus

- Machines and equipment
- Controls
- Explaining how things work
- Making offers
- Further practice: giving instructions
- Phrasal verbs (separable)
- Position of object pronoun
- Sequence word: *next*
- Further practice: imperatives

Machines around us

1 🔊 Listen and read. Karl Schiller is German. He's a friend of Julia's and he's in London to visit MAP Advertising. A hotel porter is showing him his room.

Match the numbers in the conversation with Pictures A–C.

KARL: It's cold in here. How do you turn on the heating?
PORTER: The heating *is* on, sir. But you're right. It *is* cold. There's a thermostat (1), here, on the wall. I'll turn it up.
KARL: Thank you . . . . There's something wrong with the TV. It doesn't work.
PORTER: You have to press this button (2).
KARL: Ah.
PORTER: The light switches (3) are here. This turns on your main light. And this turns on the bedside lights. And this is your radio and alarm clock.
KARL: Thank you.
PORTER: Will that be all, sir?
KARL: Yes. That's fine, thanks.
PORTER: Thank you, sir. Enjoy your stay.

2 Now complete the chart to show which verbs are used with each piece of equipment and each control.

	TURN	TURN ON/OFF	TURN UP/DOWN	PRESS
the heating the TV the radio	no	.....	.....	.....
the lights	no	.....	.....	no
the button the switch	no	no	.....	.....
the knob	yes	no	no	no

DISCOVERING LANGUAGE

3 Look again at Karl's question:
How do you turn on the heating?

Does *you* refer to:
a) a person?
b) people working in the hotel?
c) the porter?

4 Work in pairs.
Student A: Ask about the things in the top part of the chart.
Student B: Answer using the words in the bottom part of the chart.
A: *How do you turn on the heating?*
B: *You turn this knob.*

5 Find machines around you. Ask and answer.
A: *How does this calculator work? How do you turn it on?*
B: *You press this button.*

6 🔊 Listen to the sounds. What did Karl do when the porter left the room? Write sentences.
1 *He turned on the radio.*

DISCOVERING LANGUAGE

7 Look at these sentences. Two of them are incorrect (*x*). What rule can you make about the position of the noun and the object pronoun with these two-part verbs?

He turned the radio off.	✓	She turned the heating up.	✓
He turned off the radio.	✓	She turned up the heating.	✓
He turned it off.	✓	She turned it up.	✓
He turned off it.	✗	She turned up it.	✗

8 Stress and intonation. Listen and underline the main stresses. Then listen and repeat.

Turn it off.
Turn off the radio.
He turned off the radio.
He turned the radio off.

Turn it up.
Turn up the heating.
She turned up the heating.
She turned the heating up.

9 Work in pairs. Look at the pictures.

Student A: You are the person in each picture. Say what the problem is.
Student B: Offer to change the situation.

A: It's very cold.
B: I'll turn the heating up.
  I'll turn up the heating.

A: The television is too loud.
B: I'll turn it down.

10 Work with a partner. Look at the picture of a video camera. Say what it is for and then explain how to use it. Write instructions.

11 Now listen to Rosie's instructions to Alan. She is explaining how to use the video camera. Correct any mistakes in your instructions.

First ...
Next ...
Then ...
Then ...

COMPARING CULTURES

12 Read what a British person says about video cameras. Then talk about the situation in your country.

❝ A lot of families have small video cameras now and they use them to record special family events like weddings and birthdays. People also make films of their children, and some people take their cameras on holiday. Most people take photographs, though – it's easier and much cheaper. ❞

13 Use your notes from Exercise 12 on page 45 and write instructions for the use of an invention.

ENGLISH AROUND YOU

Development

SPEAKING

1 Look at these pictures of Bronco McLoughlin at work and answer the questions.
1 What is he doing in the pictures?
2 What do you think his job is?
3 What other things do you think he has to do in his work?

LISTENING

2 🔊 Now listen to Bronco talking about his work and answer the questions.
1 What does he do?
2 Which of these films did he work on?
   a) the Indiana Jones films
   b) *Rambo II*
   c) *Rambo III*
   d) *Total Recall*
   e) the James Bond films
3 Which of these film stars does he mention?
   a) Sean Connery
   b) Tom Cruise
   c) Robert de Niro
   d) Charles Bronson
   e) Julia Roberts
   f) Sylvester Stallone
   g) Arnold Schwarzenegger
   h) Richard Harris

READING

3 Read this newspaper article about Bronco. Then put these events in the correct order.
a) He worked on his first film.
b) He learned to ride.
c) He moved to England.
d) He rode wild horses in competitions.
e) He was born in Ireland.
f) He went to Australia.
g) He became a successful stuntman.
h) He returned to Ireland.
i) He got a job on a cattle ranch.

Bronco McLoughlin – twentieth-century cowboy

Bronco McLoughlin was born and brought up in Ireland. At the age of sixteen he left and went to live in Australia. 'When I was a boy, I always wanted to be a cowboy. In Australia I got a job on a cattle ranch, and that's where I learned to ride. I became a good rider and a few years later I started taking part in rodeos – riding wild horses in competitions. It was in Australia that I really learned about horses – how to look after them, and how to train them to do what you want them to do.'

In 1966, after twelve years in Australia, Bronco went home to Ireland to see his father. By chance a film company was making a film near his home. The film was called Viking Queen and they wanted a good rider to be an extra. Bronco got the job and after that, with the contacts that he made in the film, he got another one . . . and then another one. Stunts became his life. He learned to do all kinds of things that most people consider dangerous. Now he is an all-round stuntman, but he still specialises in working with horses. His home is in England, but he is away for most of the year because he works on films all over the world.

SPEAKING

4 In *Robin Hood, Prince of Thieves,* Robin Hood (Kevin Costner) shot an arrow at Bronco, who played an enemy horseman. The pictures show how Bronco does a stunt like this. Put them in the order that you think is correct. Then match the captions with the pictures.

1 Picture C – *I fix a cable to a tree.*
a) I get on my horse.
b) I hit the ground.
c) I gallop to the end of the cable.
d) I fix a cable to a tree.
e) The cable stops me in mid-air. The horse gallops on. I fall off the horse. The arrow pops up from my chest.
f) I put a harness on and attach the cable to it.

LISTENING

5 📼 Now listen to Bronco explaining how he does this stunt, and check your answers to Exercise 4.

WRITING

6 Work with a partner and write about the stunt in Exercise 4. Use the captions to help you but add other words, phrases or sentences. Use the past tense and these sequencers:

first   next   then   after that

First he fixed a cable to a tree ...

7 Now write about a stunt that you saw in a film or in real life. Write what happened and try to explain how it happened. Ask your teacher about new words that you need.

UNIT SIX

Summary

FUNCTIONAL LANGUAGE

Talking about function
What's it for?
It's for carrying food.

Giving instructions in sequence.
First, turn the shower on.
Next, stand under the shower-head.
Then move your feet on the pedals.

Explaining how something works
How does it work?
You press this button.
How do you turn on this calculator?
You press this button.

Making offers
I'll turn up the heating.

GRAMMAR

Phrasal verbs
turn on/turn off
turn up/turn down

Position of object pronoun
Turn *it* on/off.

Position of object noun
Turn *the heating* on.
Turn on *the heating*.

Imperatives (revision)
AFFIRMATIVE
Turn it on.
NEGATIVE
Don't turn it on.

See the Grammar Reference section at the back of the book for more information.

UNITS 4–6
Progress check 2

Vocabulary

1 Match the sentences with these words.
You wear it to keep your neck warm. – *a scarf*
a scarf   earrings   a tie   a belt   gloves   socks   a dress
1 You wear them on your feet.
2 Men wear one around their neck, often when they wear a suit.
3 You wear them in your ears.
4 Only women wear it.
5 You wear it around your waist to keep your trousers up.
6 You wear them on your hands in cold weather.

2 Disagree with each speaker.
'It's a large table.'
No, it isn't. It's small.
1 'These trousers are tight.'
2 'It's an ugly jacket.'
3 'Those are his smart clothes.'
4 'Your shoes are wet!'

3 Label the parts of the bicycle with these words.
wheel   seat   handlebars   lights   mirror   tyre   brake

4 Complete the sentences with these verbs.
turn on   turn up   press   pull   push
1 Please ..... the curtains across that window.
2 Can you ..... the light, please?
3 ..... the button next to the door.
4 It's cold in here. I'll ..... the heating.
5 We'll have to ..... the car to the garage.

Grammar and functions

5 Write the superlative form of these adjectives.
long – *the longest*
1 old   4 bad   7 expensive
2 dangerous   5 beautiful   8 important
3 high   6 good

6 Peter wants to find a new house. He doesn't like the area in the picture. Why not? Write sentences using *too* or *enough*.
roads: wide
The roads aren't wide enough.
1 roads: busy   4 area: quiet
2 houses: old   5 traffic: noisy
3 houses: large   6 streets: dirty

7 Complete the conversation.
ASSISTANT: Good morning. Can I help you?
CLARE: Yes, I'd like one of those T-shirts, please. A blue one.
ASSISTANT: Right. (1) ..... ?
CLARE: Medium, I think.
ASSISTANT: (2) ..... ?
CLARE: Yes, please. – Yes, this is fine. (3) ..... ?
ASSISTANT: £12.99.
CLARE: OK. (4) ......

PROGRESS CHECK 2

8 You are in a restaurant and the waiter brings you the bill below. Are these sentences true or false? Correct the false ones.
1. You have to pay the bill.
2. The total includes all taxes.
3. You have to leave a tip.
4. You can't pay by credit card.
5. You can pay by cheque.

ANNIE'S KITCHEN

Chicken Chasseur	£6.95
Gateau	£3.00
Coffee	£1.50
Total	£11.45

We accept cheques and credit cards.
Prices include VAT.
If you were happy with the service, please remember your waiter.

9 Complete the sentences with the correct form of the verb *have to*.

We usually ..... work until seven
We usually have to work until seven.

1. What time ..... the teachers ..... arrive at school in the mornings?
2. I ..... leave my job, but the work was very boring so it was a good thing really.
3. She ..... catch the ten thirty train because she missed the nine o'clock one.
4. It's OK. We're not late. We ..... be there until six thirty.
5. ..... you ..... do a lot of homework last night?

10 Write the past simple tense form of these verbs. Which verb is regular?
have – *had*
1. drive
2. do
3. lead
4. go
5. save
6. put
7. find
8. take

11 Write questions for these answers.
It's a tin opener.
What's this?

1. It's for opening tins.
2. You turn the thermostat on the wall.
3. You press this button to start it and that button to stop it.
4. It's broken.
5. No, you can't. You have to park in the car park.

12 Put these instructions for sending a letter in the correct order and add the sequence words *then*, *next* and *first* in appropriate places.

Put it in a stamped, addressed envelope.
Put the letter in a letter box.
Write your letter.

Common errors

13 Add five more missing words to correct the conversation.

Are you mechanic?
Are you a mechanic?

CUSTOMER: Are you mechanic?
MECHANIC: Yes. Can I help you?
CUSTOMER: There's something wrong the lights on my car.
MECHANIC: What the matter with them?
CUSTOMER: I don't know. They not working. Can you look them now?
MECHANIC: No, I busy at the moment.

14 Correct the word order.

It's got on it a mark.
It's got a mark on it.

1. I take shoes size six.
2. Look at those brown beautiful sandals!
3. It's the suit most expensive in the shop.
4. This coat is not enough long.
5. Here's the video recorder. You turn on it here.

15 Find the mistakes in this student text. Rewrite the text correctly.

> I think the best – and the most old – thing that I am having is a brown leather trousers. It is comfortable and it suit me. It wasn't too much expensive. I bought it from a friend and it only cost a hundred francs.

At the end of the Progress Check, look back at your mistakes and study the Grammar Reference section for further help.

7 Getting around town

Sightseeing

Focus
- Waxworks
- Taxis
- Tipping

- Describing manner
- Adverbs of manner (-ly and irregular forms)

1 Julia is showing Karl the sights of London. They are at Madame Tussaud's Waxwork Museum. Look at the pictures. Which are the models? Which are the living people?

2 Now read about the museum and answer the questions.
1 Where was Madame Tussaud from?
2 When did she open the London museum?
3 What are the models made of?
4 How long does it take to make a model?
5 Where do the clothes usually come from?
6 Why do staff replace the models?
7 What changes are they planning at the museum?

3 Find words in the text that mean:
1 a public show of objects. (Paragraph 2)
2 a group of people working together. (Paragraph 3)
3 people who make models or statues. (Paragraph 3)
4 a famous person. (Paragraph 3)

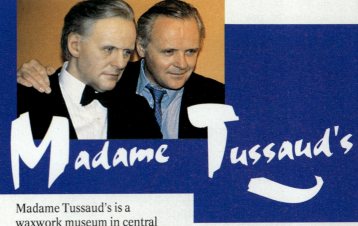

Madame Tussaud's is a waxwork museum in central London. It contains wax models of famous people, living and dead: kings and queens, film stars, politicians, pop idols and murderers. Over two million people visit the museum every year, making it Britain's number one tourist attraction.

The original Madame Tussaud lived nearly 200 years ago. She started making models in wax as a teenager and came to London from Paris in 1802. After travelling around the country with her waxwork exhibition for many years, she set up the museum in 1835. Her grandsons moved it to its present home fifty years later.

The team of full-time sculptors at Madame Tussaud's cannot work fast but they do their job well, and the models are amazingly lifelike. The celebrity visits the museum first to meet the sculptor, who takes hundreds of photographs and measurements. The celebrity usually provides clothes for the model to wear. Each model takes about six months to complete because the sculptors have to work slowly and carefully. They make the eyes separately and put real human hair into the wax one hair at a time. 'It's important that people recognise the models. When celebrities are no longer popular, we replace the model quickly,' says a spokesperson.

Madame Tussaud's changes with the times. In the future, with the use of computer technology, the museum is planning to show figures that can walk and talk. ■

52

DISCOVERING LANGUAGE

4 Complete the chart with some of the adverbs from the text. Make a rule about forming regular adverbs from adjectives.

REGULAR		IRREGULAR	
Adjective	Adverb	Adjective	Adverb
slow	*slowly*	good	.....
careful	.....	fast	.....
quick	.....		

5 Complete the sentences with one of these adverbs.

beautifully   hard   dangerously   well   politely
easily   badly   carefully   quietly   fast

1 She never has accidents. She drives .....
2 What a lovely picture! He paints .....
3 She's good at her job. She works .....
4 The exam wasn't difficult. He finished it .....
5 I can't hear her. She speaks so .....

6 Work with a partner. Think of an action that you can describe with each of the adverbs in the list in Exercise 5. Write sentences.

She sings beautifully.

7 📼 Word stress. Listen to the adverbs from the list that end in *-ly* and underline the stressed syllables. Make a rule about stress on the *-ly* ending. Then listen and repeat.

8 📼 Julia and Karl are now looking for a taxi to take Karl back to his hotel. Listen and answer the questions.
1 What colour are most London taxis?
2 What is a tip?
3 How much do British taxi drivers usually expect as a tip?

🌀 COMPARING CULTURES

9 Read these statements about registered London taxis. Are they true for taxis in your town or city?
1 You can stop a taxi in the street by raising your hand.
2 The taxi driver has to take you where you want to go.
3 It is unusual to share a taxi with a stranger.
4 Taxis are safe, even at night.
6 You pay the price on the meter.

10 Where are the taxis in the pictures from? Match them with the countries below and give reasons for your choices. Which is most similar to taxis in your country?

1 – India. I think it's from the India because I have a book about India with photos like this.

India   Britain   the United States   Indonesia

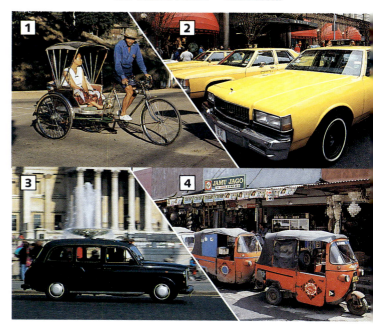

11 You give a 'tip', or extra money, to someone who does a job well for you. Look at the chart below. It shows the people who usually get tips in Britain. Then answer the questions.
1 Which people get tips in your country? Complete the second column of the chart.
2 Ten per cent (10 %) is an average tip in Britain. What about in your country?
3 Some people feel that giving tips is wrong. What do you think?

TIPPING	Britain	Your country
Taxi driver	Yes	.....
Waiter	Yes	.....
Postman	No	.....
Builder	No	.....
Car park attendant	No	.....
Cinema employee	No	.....
Hotel porter	Yes	.....
Cloakroom attendant (e.g. in a theatre)	Yes	.....
Tourist guide	Yes	.....

Getting to work

1 🎧 Rosie Brady is visiting her brother in London. Listen and write James's answers to Rosie's questions.

ROSIE: How do you get to work?
How far is it?
How long does it take you?
And how much does it cost?

2 Ask your partner about his/her journey to school or work. Write the answers and then tell the class.

Pia comes to school by bus. It's about five kilometres and the journey takes twenty-five minutes. It costs 2,000 lire.

3 Look at the photographs. They show other ways of getting to work. Say what you think about them. Make comparisons.

4 Work in pairs.
Student A: Read the articles below and match them with two of the pictures. Then ask your partner questions about the journeys in the other pictures.
How ... ?   How far ... ?
How long ... ?   How much ... ?
Student B: Turn to page 118. Read the other two articles. Answer your partner.

A Chris Grunwell rows his own boat half a mile to work because it's quicker than driving. If he drives, the journey is two miles longer and takes over thirty minutes in heavy traffic. The twenty-minute boat trip is good exercise. Chris arrives at work feeling fit and healthy, and it doesn't cost him anything!

B Australian Geoff Watchorn, director of a company in south London, travels to central London by helicopter and then to his office by bicycle. He drove to work for seven years, but after a road accident he bought the helicopter for £60,000. His thirty-mile journey now takes him twenty minutes instead of one and a half hours, and the cost of running the helicopter is only ten per cent more than the cost of using his car.

Focus

- Means of transport
- Times and distances
- Maps and directions

- Talking about distance, time and frequency
- Giving directions

- Questions:
  How far?
  How long?
  How much?
  How often?

UNIT SEVEN

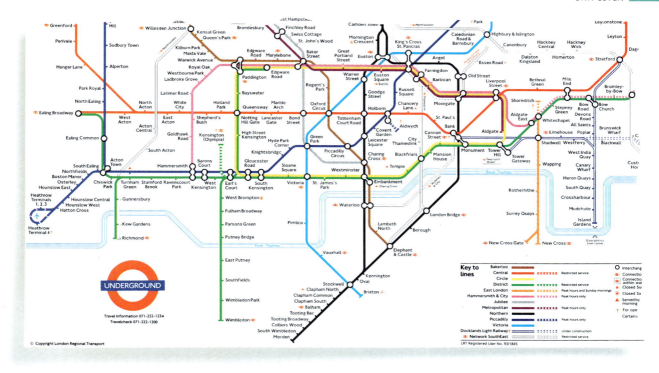

5 🔲 The plan above shows part of the London Underground (tube) system. Find Wimbledon underground station on the plan. Then listen to a conversation between James and Rosie. Follow the journey on the plan and name the nearest underground station to MAP Advertising, where James works.

6 🔲 Listen again. Note how to get from James's flat to MAP Advertising. Then work with a partner and write directions for Rosie. Start like this:

Go out of the house and turn ...

7 🔲 Stress and intonation. Listen. Underline the main stresses in this sentence.

Excuse me. How do I get to Madame Tussaud's?

Now listen and repeat.
1 Excuse me. How do I get to Trafalgar Square?
2 Excuse me. How do I get to Buckingham Palace?
3 Excuse me. How do I get to the Hard Rock Café?
4 Excuse me. How do I get to the Tate Gallery?

8 Work in pairs.
Student A: You are at Holborn underground station. You have a tube map. Explain how to get to famous places by underground.
Student B: Turn to page 119. Ask for directions to famous places.
B: *Excuse me. How do I get to Madame Tussaud's?*
A: *What's the nearest underground station to Madame Tussaud's?*
B: *Er... I think the nearest station's Baker Street.*
A: *Right. Take the Central Line to Oxford Circus, then change to the Jubilee Line. Get off at Baker Street.*

9 Match each question with two possible answers. Then ask and answer about places near your home.
1 How far is (the station)?
2 How long does (the journey) take?
3 How often do (the buses) go?
4 How much is (the fare)?

   a) A long time.   f) A lot.
   b) Not far.   g) Not very often.
   c) Not much.
   d) Quite often.   h) Not long.
   e) A long way.

ENGLISH AROUND YOU

Development

READING

1 You are in London and you want to go on a boat trip. Read the brochure and find the answers to the questions.
1. How long does the trip take?
2. What is the name of the nearest underground station?
3. Which buses stop near the place of departure? Give the bus numbers.
4. How much is a return journey for:
   a) an adult and a fifteen-year-old?
   b) two adults and two children aged four and two?

SPEAKING

2 Work in pairs. You decide to go on Jason's Trip but you are not sure how to get to the boat.
Student A: Ask your partner how to get to the boat by underground. You are staying near Bond Street station. Your partner will give you directions. Make notes.
Student B: Turn to page 119. Use the maps to give your partner directions.

LISTENING

3 🔊 Paul Money takes tourists on trips in one of Jason's boats. Listen and match these places with the numbers on the map below:

Camden Town   Little Venice   London Zoo
Maida Hill Tunnel

JASON'S TRIP
LITTLE VENICE LONDON

Enjoy a fascinating one and a half hour trip on a traditional, gaily painted narrow boat along the Regent's Canal. London's original canal cruise with over 40 year's experience.

INFORMATION

Our boarding place is opposite 60 Blomfield Road, Little Venice, less than three minutes walk from Warwick Avenue underground station and bus routes 6 and 46 which stop there.

TRIP TIMES

April–October   10.30, 12.30, 2.30
Arrival and departure at Camden Lock 11.15, 1.15, 3.15

FARES

	Return	One way
Adult	£4.50	£3.50
Child (14 & under)	£3.25	£2.50

Family return ticket (2 adults & 2 children) £14
Children 3 and under are free.

Telephone 071 286 3428 Fax 071 266 4332

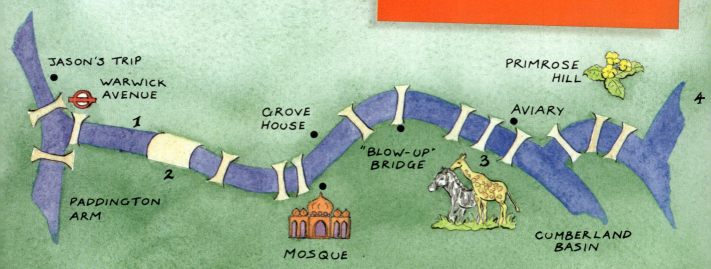

4 🔊 **Listen again and answer the questions.**
1. How far is Hampstead Road Lock from Little Venice?
2. Who are Paul Money's favourite passengers:
   a) children?   b) teenagers?   c) older people?
3. What is the speed limit for boats on the Regent's Canal?
4. Which of these animals can you see when you pass London Zoo:
   a) lions?   c) bears?   e) elephants?
   b) antelopes?   d) tigers?
5. What does he like about his job? Which of these does he mention:
   a) the money?   c) the working hours?   e) fishing?
   b) the boats?   d) the fresh air?   f) meeting people?

WRITING

5 You went on the trip and bought a postcard of the boat. Write to an English friend telling him/her about the trip and the things that you saw. Continue the postcard below.

April 15th

Dear
We went on a great
boat trip yesterday.

UNIT SEVEN

Summary

FUNCTIONAL LANGUAGE

Talking about directions
How do I get to the Tower of London?
Take the Central Line to Monument, then change to the District Line and get off at Tower Hill.

Talking about distance
How far is it?
Five miles. / A long way. / Not far.

Talking about time
How long does it take (you)?
Forty-five minutes. /
A long time. / Not long.

Talking about frequency
How often do the buses go?
Quite often. / Not very often.

Talking about manner
I drive very carefully.

GRAMMAR

Question words
How far?
How long?
How often?
How much?

Adverbs
REGULAR
adjective + *ly*:
slow – slowly
IRREGULAR
fast – fast
good – well
hard – hard

See the Grammar Reference section at the back of the book for more information.

8 Cooking a meal

Shopping for food

Focus
- Supermarkets
- Food and household goods
- Prices

- Asking polite questions
- Saying what someone has to pay
- Asking about forms of payment
- Asking about quantity

- Indirect (polite) questions
- *Some* and *any*
- Countable and uncountable nouns
- Questions: *How much? How many?*

1 Teresa is at a supermarket. Look at the labels below for the different sections of the supermarket. Then look at the things in Teresa's shopping basket and say in which section she found each item.

She found the ice cream in the 'Frozen desserts' section.

Frozen desserts   Meat   Bakery   Sweets
Cooking ingredients   Dairy products
Vegetables   Body and hair care
Canned food   General household goods

2 Work in pairs. Look at Teresa's shopping basket and add the items to her shopping list below.

Student A: Ask about quantities. Your partner has got the complete list.
Student B: Look at page 120 and answer your partner's questions.

A: *How much ice cream has Teresa got?*
B: *She's got two litres.*
A: *How many carrots has she got?*

Student A: Now ask what else Teresa needs, and complete the list.

A: *What else does she need?*
B: *She needs some flour.*
A: *How much flour does she need?*

Shopping list
2 litres of ice cream
*   of carrots*

3  Listen. Teresa is talking to a shop assistant. Say what Teresa wants and where the items are.

4  Listen again. Complete Teresa's two questions.

TERESA: Can you tell me .....?

DISCOVERING LANGUAGE

5 Look at the pairs of questions below. Which question in each pair is more polite? What is the difference between the verb forms in each pair?

1 a) How much **is** this?
   b) Can you tell me how much this **is**?
2 a) How much **does** it **cost**?
   b) Can you tell me how much it **costs**?
3 a) How **do** you **cook** this?
   b) Can you tell me how you **cook** this?

Now look at the questions below. There are no question words in the simple questions. Which word do we add when we form a polite question?

4 a) Are there any peas?
   b) Can you tell me if there are any peas?
5 a) Have you got any tomatoes?
   b) Can you tell me if you've got any tomatoes?

6 Stress and intonation. Listen and repeat.

Can you …?
Can you tell me …?
Can you tell me where the …?
Can you tell me where the carrots are?

Now listen and repeat this question.

Can you …?
Can you tell me …?
Can you tell me if there's …?
Can you tell me if there's any bread?

7 Work in pairs.

Student A: Look again at your list from Exercise 2. Ask your partner polite questions about where the things are in the supermarket.
Student B: Look at the section labels in Exercise 1 and answer your partner.

A: *Excuse me. Can you tell me where the flour is?*
B: *Yes. It's in the 'Cooking ingredients' section.*

8 Work in pairs and then change A and B roles.

Student A: Look at the pictures. Ask polite questions using the words and phrases.
Student B: You are the shop assistant. Look at page 120. Answer the questions.

9 Stress and intonation. Listen and repeat. Teresa is checking the things in her shopping basket.

… ice cream, lamb, carrots, milk and chocolates.

Now practise saying these lists. Then check with the cassette. Listen again and repeat.

1 I need some cheese, some eggs, some flour and a loaf of bread.
2 Some sugar, some biscuits, and a packet of tea.
3 Jam, marmalade, butter and milk.

10 Listen to Teresa's conversation with the assistant at the check-out. Correct the mistakes in the conversation below.

ASSISTANT: That's £14.20, please. How are you paying?
TERESA: Cash … Here you are.
ASSISTANT: Thank you. Here's your change. Do you need any more bags?
TERESA: Yes, two more, please. Thank you. Goodbye.
ASSISTANT: Goodbye.

The food we eat

1 Read what four people say about the food they like best. Find adjectives to describe food that:
1 is not frozen or in cans.
2 is uncooked.
3 is good for your body.
4 is bad for your body.
5 has sugar in it.
6 is cooked in a lot of oil.
7 tastes terrible.
8 makes you fat.

Focus

- Food and its characteristics
- Saying what you think
- Responding to argument

- *A lot (of), (not) much* and *(not) many*
- Question: *What kind?*
- Further practice: *How much? How many? some, any*

1 " I eat a lot of fresh fruit and raw vegetables. They're healthy and they taste good. I'm not keen on sweet things and I don't eat much fatty food. "

2 " I'm afraid I'm keen on junk food – you know, quick, unhealthy food like hamburgers or chips. A lot of people think it's revolting, but I like it. I don't eat many fresh vegetables. "

3 " Crisps are my favourite, I suppose. I know they're bad for you, but they're delicious – especially cheese and onion ones. "

4 " I love sweet things like cakes and chocolates. I know they aren't good for me and they're fattening, but I can't resist them! "

DISCOVERING LANGUAGE

2 Look again at the comments above. Make rules for the use of *much, many, a lot (of)*.

3 Ask your partner questions to complete the questionnaire below.
A: *What kind of food are you keen on?*
B: *I'm very keen on junk food/sweet things.*
A: *How much/many do you eat each week?*
B: *I eat a lot of junk food, but I don't eat many sweet things because they're bad for my teeth.*

4 Write about your partner.
Gina is very keen on junk food and sweet things. She eats a lot of hamburgers and chips and she loves cakes and chocolates. She doesn't eat much fruit and she's not very keen on salads and vegetables. I don't think her diet is very healthy.

VERY KEEN	QUITE KEEN	NOT VERY KEEN	HATE		NOT ANY	NOT MUCH/ MANY	SOME	A LOT
yes	.....	.....	.....	Junk food	.....	.....	.....	.....
.....	.....	.....	.....	Meat	.....	.....	.....	.....
.....	.....	.....	.....	Vegetables	.....	.....	.....	.....
.....	.....	.....	.....	Salads	.....	.....	.....	.....
.....	.....	.....	.....	Fresh fruit	.....	.....	.....	.....
.....	.....	.....	.....	Dairy produce	.....	.....	.....	.....
.....	.....	.....	.....	Sweet things	.....	.....	.....	.....

UNIT EIGHT

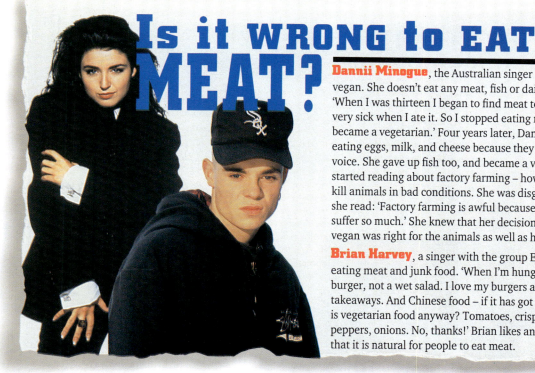

Is it WRONG to EAT MEAT?

Dannii Minogue, the Australian singer and actress, is a vegan. She doesn't eat any meat, fish or dairy products. 'When I was thirteen I began to find meat too fatty. I felt very sick when I ate it. So I stopped eating meat and became a vegetarian.' Four years later, Dannii stopped eating eggs, milk, and cheese because they were bad for her voice. She gave up fish too, and became a vegan. Then she started reading about factory farming – how we keep and kill animals in bad conditions. She was disgusted by what she read: 'Factory farming is awful because the animals suffer so much.' She knew that her decision to become a vegan was right for the animals as well as herself.

Brian Harvey, a singer with the group East 17, enjoys eating meat and junk food. 'When I'm hungry I want a big burger, not a wet salad. I love my burgers and fried chicken takeaways. And Chinese food – if it has got meat in it. What is vegetarian food anyway? Tomatoes, crispy lettuce, green peppers, onions. No, thanks!' Brian likes animals but feels that it is natural for people to eat meat.

5 Read the article above and answer these questions.
1 What is the difference between their eating habits?
2 What can't a vegetarian eat? What can't a vegan eat?

6 Match the arguments on the left with the reasons that support them.

Eating meat is:
1 unkind
2 natural
3 unnecessary
4 unhealthy

a) You can get protein, iron and vitamins from vegetarian food. You don't need to eat meat.
b) The animals that people eat have terrible lives.
c) Meat-eaters have 30 per cent more problems with heart disease than vegetarians.
d) People eat meat all over the world. It is a normal part of a lot of people's diet.

7 Work in pairs.
Student A: List other arguments for being a vegetarian.
Student B: List other arguments for eating meat.
Convince your partner. Use these expressions to help you:
I think/I feel …   I agree, but …
I'm sorry, I don't agree.   You're right, but …
That's true, but …   I don't think that's true.

A: *I think eating meat is wrong because …*
B: *I'm sorry, I don't agree. There's nothing wrong with eating meat …*

COMPARING CULTURES

8 Look at the pictures below. Think about the food people eat in your country and other countries that you know. Then complete these sentences.

1 A lot of people in (*Brazil*) eat … because …
2 Not many people in (*Japan*) eat … because …

snails, bacon, sweets, ants, lobster, cream, seaweed, snakes, lettuce

61

Development

LISTENING

1 🔊 Dennis Malone and his wife are the owners of Milly's Restaurant in San Rafael, California. They prepare healthy, vegetarian meals. They never use meat, butter, cream, oil or eggs. Listen to Dennis talking about his popular speciality, O'Malley's Stew. Put these cooking instructions in the right order.

1 Add the Shii-taki mushrooms and the smoked tofu.

2 Add the fresh herbs and let the stew simmer.

3 Chop the vegetables.

4 Blanch the carrots and leeks, then simmer them.

5 Wash the vegetables.

6 Add the remaining ingredients.

A

~THE LOTUS~
Chinese cuisine in Oxfordshire
77 Millet Street • Oxford • OX1 4QP

SPECIAL SUMMER OFFER
Seafood set dinner – £19.95 including lobster

✤ Healthy eating special – a treat for vegetarians
✤ Dim Sum traditional Chinese Brunch
available from Sunday to Thursday
and lots more to choose from every Sunday lunchtime only
~ Telephone 0865 249249 ~

B

The Coach and Four
Chislehampton, Oxford
Telephone (0865) 830244

XVIth CENTURY RESTAURANT

Table d'hôte, extensive à la carte and vegetarian menus available at dinner Monday to Saturday, and lunch Monday to Friday.
Traditional roast lunch served Sundays (12–2 pm).
A main course, two courses or the full menu – the choice is yours. Vegetarians are welcome.
'Fax your order menu' available weekday lunchtimes.

READING

2 Look at the newspaper advertisements for restaurants. Which restaurants:
1 serve lunch on Sundays?
2 serve meals on Monday evenings?
3 serve vegetarian food?
4 serve food from other countries?
5 take lunch orders by fax?

3 Say which restaurant is the best for these groups of people.
1 Julie, Robert and their children want to eat food that is not English. Julie is a strict vegetarian who does not eat meat or fish.
2 Pablo and Graziella want to have lunch outside and listen to music.
3 Dieter and Hans want to try a traditional English Sunday lunch in an old restaurant.
4 Sally and Mike don't want much food, but they would like to have tea and cakes in an unusual kind of restaurant.

THE MATILDA — ENJOY OXFORD'S CRUISING RESTAURANT

Open for lunch and dinner

Also available for party bookings, champagne breakfast, cream teas, lunch, dinner or conferences – up to 28 passengers · Evening dinner cruises Wednesday – Saturday and Sunday lunch · Cream teas any day

Please phone for full details and reservations
TEL: OXFORD 59976

THE WATERMILL

IT'S ALL HAPPENING AT THE MILL!

Lunch time barbecues
Every Saturday and Sunday · Riverside Barbecues

JAZZ AT THE MILL
At lunch times on last Sunday each month.
Come and join us.
For further details and reservations
telephone Oxford 54179

LISTENING

4 Listen. Someone from Exercise 3 is phoning a restaurant. Who is it? Which restaurant?

5 Listen again and complete these sentences and questions from the conversation.
1 I'd like .....
2 Would you like .....?
3 Do you serve .....?
4 And can you tell me .....?

SPEAKING

6 Work in pairs.
Student A: Phone one of the restaurants above. Ask for more information and make a reservation.
Student B: You are the manager. Take a reservation and note the day, the time and the number of people.

WRITING

7 Write a paragraph explaining why you are or are not a vegetarian.

Summary

FUNCTIONAL LANGUAGE

Asking polite questions
Can you tell me how much it costs?
Can you tell me if there's any bread?

Saying what a person has to pay
That's fourteen pounds twenty, please.

Asking about ways of paying
How are you paying?
Cash./By cheque.

Asking about quantity
How much (meat) does she need?
Not much./A lot./A kilo.
How many (bags) does she need?
Not many./A lot./Five.

Saying what you think
I think (that) meat-eating is cruel.
I feel (that) a vegetarian diet is healthier.

Responding to an argument
I agree./I'm sorry, I don't agree.
That's true./I don't think that's true.
You're right./I'm afraid you're wrong.

GRAMMAR

Indirect polite questions

| Can you tell me | how much / when / how / where / if | + subject + verb |

***How much/ many* (revision)**
how much + uncountable noun
how many + countable noun

***Much, many, a lot (of)* (revision)**
(not) much + uncountable noun
(not) many + countable noun
a lot of + uncountable/countable noun

See the Grammar Reference section at the back of the book for more information.

9 In the country

Focus

- Locations
- Country and city life
- Talking about location
- Saying what is best
- Further practice: asking for and giving opinions, making comparisons

- Modal: *should* + infinitive
- Further practice: comparative adjectives

Changing places

1 Look at the map below. It shows places where people live. Then answer the questions.
1 Where do you live?
   I live in a village in the north of France.
2 Where's your school?
   It's in the suburbs of Paris.
3 Where are the nearest big shops?
   They're in the city centre.

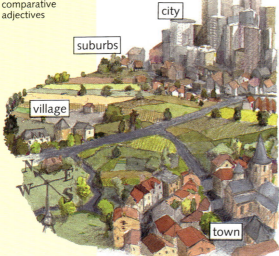

3 Read the first paragraph of the article below about a family who live in the country. Correct these sentences.
1 They live in a house.
2 They stay in one place.
3 The child goes to school.
4 Her father wants to return to the city.

2 Work with a partner. Ask and answer about family, work and other places that are important to you.
Where do your grandparents live?
Where do your parents work?

Terry, aged twenty-eight, is typical of one kind of New Age Traveller. Before she went on the road, she and her husband, Streak, lived with their small daughter in one room in a big city. They did a series of boring, badly-paid jobs and were poor and unhappy. Then some friends offered them a van to live in. For two years they moved around the country with other travellers, parking on public land. Now their daughter, Scarlet, is four years old and Terry wants to move back to the city so that Scarlet can go to school. But Streak likes the travelling life. He thinks that they should stay on the road.

❝We've got a lot of good friends here. We live in the open air, we keep animals ... we do what we want to do. If we like a place, we stay for a time. If we don't like it, we move on. I hate cities. You have to live in a little box and you spend all your time doing a terrible job just to get enough money to stay alive. That's not living, it's just surviving. I think we should stay away from cities. Scarlet doesn't need to go to school. She can learn real things about life with us on the road. She's with people who love her, a long way away from the dangers of growing up in the city.❞

UNIT NINE

4 Now read the whole article. Answer the questions.
1. Who is speaking in the second and third paragraphs? How do you know?
2. Complete the chart with the points that the speakers make.

	GOOD POINTS	BAD POINTS
Travelling life	good friends	.....
City life	.....	.....

5 Read the opinions of different lifestyles below. Ask and answer. Give reasons for your answers.
1. 'Life is more interesting in the city.'
   A: **Is** life interesting in the city?
   B: I think so./I don't think so...
2. 'Children are safer in the country.'
3. 'A school education is important.'
4. 'Living in a van is very hard.'
5. 'Country life is healthier than city life.'

'Yes, travelling is fun in the spring and summer, but winter is always difficult. Scarlet gets ill every winter and she has a bad cough for most of the year. I like this life better than living in a city, but I think that Scarlet should decide what she wants. We shouldn't stop her going to school. She needs a good education and she should have friends who lead a 'normal' life. Unfortunately, that means we have to live in one place. We can't keep travelling forever anyway, and problems with farmers and police make life difficult. Streak and I talk about it all the time. Should we move back to the city or shouldn't we? I know what I want to do.'

DISCOVERING LANGUAGE

6 Find sentences in the article containing the words *should* and *shouldn't*. Then make sentences from the words below to show the correct position of *should/shouldn't*.

AFFIRMATIVE
think move the I we to should city that

NEGATIVE
keep travelling shouldn't we

INTERROGATIVE
Scarlet school go should to

Now complete the sentence to describe the function of *should*.
The speaker is:
a) making a decision.
b) saying what he/she thinks is best.
c) saying what is definitely going to happen.

7 Work in pairs. Use your chart from Exercise 4. Discuss what you think the family should do and give reasons.
Student A: You are Streak. **Student B:** You are Terry.
A: I think we should stay here in the van. Scarlet likes it and she's got a lot of friends.
B: I agree with you, but.../It isn't true that.../I'm sorry, but I don't agree with you...

8 Work in pairs. Tom Hall is having a meeting with James and Julia to discuss the possibility of moving MAP Advertising to a small country town. Listen and then recreate the discussion.
Student A: As you listen, note down the advantages of the move. Then take Tom's role.
Student B: Note the disadvantages of moving. Then take Julia's role.

9 You receive a letter from an English friend. She is thinking of moving to your area, and wants information and advice. Write a reply. Start in the same way as the letter below (but use your own address and town) and then continue like this:

PARAGRAPH 2 Describe where you live.
PARAGRAPH 3 Describe the advantages of living there.
PARAGRAPH 4 Describe the disadvantages.
PARAGRAPH 5 Say what you think your friend should do.
ENDING   Say that you hope to hear from your friend again soon.

Via Marconi 16
Rome
Italy

April 8th

Dear Penny,
Thanks for your letter. I am happy to hear that you are thinking about moving to Rome. Let me tell you something about my area. I live in...

Pets or pests?

⟳ COMPARING CULTURES

1 Look at the pictures of the most popular pets in Britain and answer the questions.
1 Which animals are common pets in your country?
2 Which pets would you not like in your house? Say why.
3 Why do you think people keep pets?

Focus

- Pets
- Asking questions
- Checking information
- Tag questions

2 Work in pairs.
Student A: Read the newspaper article (Text 1). Then read the questions next to your text. For each question, choose the answer that matches the writer's opinion.
Student B: Read the letter to a newspaper (Text 2). Then read the questions next to your text. For each question, choose the answer that matches the writer's opinion.

1 Tropical fish
2 Goldfish
3 Cats
4 Dogs
5 Budgerigars ('Budgies')
6 Hamsters
7 Rabbits
8 Guinea pigs

TEXT 1

Furry friends are good for your health

New research shows that dog and cat owners have fewer heart attacks than other people.

Doctors already knew that we become calmer when we stroke an animal and that walking a dog is good, regular exercise. But a new study of 5,700 people shows that people with cats and dogs have lower cholesterol and blood pressure levels – in other words, they are generally healthier.

Some doctors are now telling patients with heart problems to get a pet. But it has to be a certain kind of pet because what is important is the physical contact and the love that passes between the pet and its owner. The love of a cat or a dog for its owner seems to be unlimited.

TEXT 2

Dear Sir,

I am writing to say how shocked I am by the amount of money that people in Britain spend on their pets. A recent article in your newspaper informed us that last year Britons spent £660,000,000 on dog food and £516,000,000 on food for their cats!

Are we completely mad? Every day we see pictures on the television news of <u>people</u> who have no food at all. A few pounds will buy them food for a week. Even in Britain there are many people without work and homes. A little money could make a big difference to them, couldn't it? But it seems that in Britain animals come first. Perhaps it is time to think again.

Yours faithfully,
Ms D. Walker

3 Tell your partner what your text says and ask about his/hers. Then read the questions next to your partner's text and choose the best answers. Finally, say what *you* think about keeping pets.

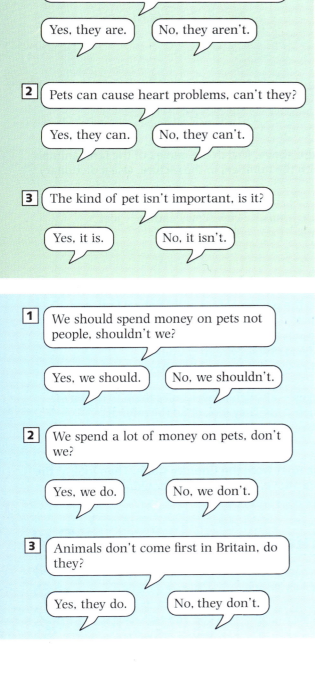

DISCOVERING LANGUAGE

4 Look at the questions in Exercise 2.
1 Read each one *without* the question tag at the end. Is it a question now?

STATEMENT	QUESTION TAG
People with cats or dogs are healthier than other people,	aren't they?

2 Find the verb in the statement and the verb in the question tag. What is the difference between them?
3 Discuss these questions with your partner. Make rules for forming question tags.
   a) You like him, don't you?
   b) He doesn't eat meat, does he?
   c) The weather's bad, isn't it?
   d) She shouldn't go, should she?
   e) They arrived late, didn't they?
   f) You can't speak Italian, can you?
   g) I haven't got the tickets, have I?

5 Now complete these questions with the correct question tag.
1 We don't spend much on cat food, ...?
2 She isn't getting a dog, ...?
3 We should give more to charity, ...?
4 You're an animal-lover, ...?
5 They lost their hamster, ...?
6 He can't afford a pet, ...?
7 It's a beautiful animal, ...?

6 🔊 Stress and intonation. We use question tags for two main reasons:
a) when we are not sure about the answer.
b) to check something we think is true.

Listen to an example of each. Does the speaker's voice go up or down at the end of each question tag? Make a rule.

1 [not sure] You're coming on Friday, aren't you?
2 [checking] Your birthday's today, isn't it?

7 🔊 Listen to the conversations. Are the questions below like 1 or 2 in Exercise 6?
1 You've got a dog, haven't you?
2 You bought some food, didn't you?
3 That's her cat, isn't it?
4 He hates animals, doesn't he?

Now listen to the questions again and repeat.

Development

READING

1 Read the extract from a magazine article below and answer the questions.
1 What two questions did the writer ask children?
2 What did the children answer?
3 Why was the writer surprised?
4 What reason does the writer give for the children's answers?

WHERE DOES MILK COME FROM?

From the supermarket of course!

That's the answer I got from a lot of the eight-year-old children in a Birmingham primary school last week. My next question was 'Where do eggs come from?', and about half the class gave the same answer. City children today know very little about where their food comes from. And how can they know? They don't see many trees, they don't see the seasons change, and they don't have any experience of animals in their natural surroundings.

SPEAKING

2 Discuss these questions with a partner.
1 Is it true in your country that some children never go outside the city?
2 Is it important?

3 Look at the picture above. Match the names of the farm animals and birds below with the numbers in the picture. Use a dictionary to help you.

duck – 1

duck   goose (geese)   horse   cow (cows/cattle)   goat
sheep (sheep)   lamb   pig   chicken/hen

LISTENING

4 🔊 **Cherry Trees Farm is a working farm in Britain that is open to visitors. Listen to the owners, Mary and Michael Bell, and answer the questions.**
1 Which of the animals in the picture do they keep on their farm?
2 Who visits their farm? Where are they from?
3 How do the visitors spend their day? Put these in the correct order:
   a) They collect eggs.   c) Michael welcomes them to the farm.
   b) They have lunch.   d) They look at all the animals.

READING

5 Read some of the rules from the Country Code. Then look at the people in the picture above. What should/shouldn't they do?
They should keep their dogs under control.

THE COUNTRY CODE
1 Enjoy the countryside and respect its life and work.
2 Keep your dogs under control.
3 Don't drop litter.
4 Be careful with fires.
5 Don't walk on fields where crops are growing.
6 Close gates behind you.
7 Don't damage hedges, fences and walls.
8 Keep away from farm animals.
9 Protect trees and plants.

UNIT NINE

Summary

FUNCTIONAL LANGUAGE

Talking about location
I live in the north/south/east/west of England.

Giving advice/Saying what's best
I think we should move to the country.
MAP shouldn't leave London.

Asking for and giving opinions
Is it safer in the country?
I think so./I don't think so.

Agreeing with someone
I agree (with you).

Disagreeing with someone
I don't agree (with you).
It isn't true that . . .

GRAMMAR

Modal: *should*
I/you/he/she/it/we/they *should* + infinitive

Question tags
You *'re* French, *aren't* you?
She *lives* there, *doesn't* she?
He *isn't* coming, *is* he?
They *can* be here tonight, *can't* they?
You *should* work harder, *shouldn't* you?

READING AND SPEAKING

6 Read the article below about a problem that is common in cities. Say what the problem is and what Sally is going to do now.

Sally will have to sleep away from home!

Last Friday a judge told noisy Sally Carter that she will go to prison if she spends one more night in her home, because she makes so much noise.

Sally, from Primrose Hill in London, kept her neighbours awake when she turned her television up too high. The neighbours and local council officials asked her 77 times to turn the television down, but she refused to listen. After the judge's decision, Sally decided to sell her flat and move to another area.

'I'll have to go somewhere else – where I can make as much noise as I like,' she said. ∎

7 Work with a partner. Discuss a 'City Code'. What rules do you think are necessary for people living near each other in flats and houses? Here are some words to give you ideas:

noise   litter   animals   children   smoking   public transport
I think people should be very quiet/shouldn't make any noise after 11 p.m.

WRITING

8 Write your City Code. Use imperative forms like the ones in the Country Code above. Then show it to another pair of students for their comments. Make changes that you agree are a good idea.

See the Grammar Reference section at the back of the book for more information.

UNITS 7–9

Progress check 3

Vocabulary

1 Which of the products below are:

1 vegetables?   4 dairy products?
2 fruit?   5 sweets?
3 meat?   6 for body or hair care?

1 vegetables: *carrots,* …

carrots   potatoes   shampoo   tissues   yoghurt
beef   soap   ice cream   toothpaste   peas
chocolates   cucumber   lamb   apples   milk
tomatoes   bananas

2 Look at the map and complete the sentences.

Perugia is in the ..... of Italy.
Perugia is in the centre of Italy.

1 Rome is in the ..... of Italy.
2 Milan is in the ..... of Italy.
3 Pescara is in the ..... of Italy.
4 Reggio di Calabria is in the
  ..... of Italy.

3 Look at the list of animals below. Find:

1 four birds.
2 an animal that lives in water all the time.
3 three animals that give milk.
4 an animal that people ride.
5 a very small animal with hair on its body.

1 *duck,* …

goldfish   cow   horse   duck   goose   chicken
sheep   budgerigar   hamster   goat

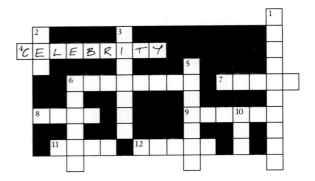

4 Use the clues to complete the crossword.

ACROSS
4 A very famous person.
6 An artist who makes models and other figures.
7 Full of fat.
8 The underground system in London.
9 Things that people do not want and throw on the ground.
11 A plant product that a farmer grows.
12 A machine in a taxi that tells you the fare.

DOWN
1 A person who never eats meat.
2 An animal that you keep in your home.
3 A place smaller than a town.
5 You use this in a supermarket.
6 A part of a town or city outside the centre.
10 Extra money that you give for good service.

Grammar and functions

5 Write the adverbs from these adjectives.

slow – *slowly*

1 quick   3 easy   5 fast   7 bad
2 good   4 careful   6 hard   8 quiet

6 Complete the conversation.

A: (1) ..... to work?
B: Oh, I usually go by bus.
A: (2) ..... ?
B: It's nine or ten kilometres.
A: (3) ..... ?
B: Usually about half an hour.

70

7 Write these questions in a more polite form.
What's the time?
Can you tell me what the time is, please?
1 How far is the centre?
  Can you tell me ..... ?
2 When does the bank open?
  Can you tell me ..... ?
3 How do I get to Oxford Circus?
  Can you tell me ..... ?
4 How much does a large tin cost?
  Can you tell me ..... ?
5 Is there a train to Paris this morning?
  Can you tell me ..... ?

8 Look at the two questions. Which words in the list below can complete Question 1? Which words can complete Question 2?
1 How much ..... have you got?
2 How many ..... have you got?
1 fruit, ...   2 mushrooms, ...
fruit   mushrooms   eggs   oranges
cheese   flour   carrots   milk   tomatoes
boxes of chocolates   bread

9 Add *should* to each of these statements and questions.
We stay in the country.
We should stay in the country.
1 I think we move to the city.
2 The little girl go to school?
3 We not keep travelling.
4 Children be near their grandparents?
5 You look ill. You see a doctor.

10 Complete each conversation with one of these phrases.
I agree.   I'm sorry, I don't agree.
You're right.   That isn't true.
1 A: I think eating meat is wrong.
  B: ...... There's nothing wrong with it.
2 A: Eating meat is unhealthy.
  B: ...... Meat-eaters have 30 per cent more problems with heart disease than vegetarians.
3 A: Eating animals isn't natural.
  B: ...... People in most countries eat meat if they can.
4 A: Eating meat is unkind to animals.
  B: ...... Animals kept for meat have terrible lives.
5 A: There's no protein in vegetarian food.
  B: ...... You can get protein in your diet without eating meat.

11 Change these statements into questions by adding question tags.
It's cold today, ...
It's cold today, isn't it?
1 British people like cats, ... ?
2 You're coming on Saturday, ... ?
3 She's late, ... ?
4 They didn't phone, ... ?
5 He can swim, ... ?
6 We shouldn't arrive before eight, ... ?

Common errors

12 Correct the spelling mistakes.
I rifuse to listen to your arguments. – *refuse*
1 We're going to an exibition of modern paintings.
2 What would you like for desert?
3 A pound of potatos and some onions, please.
4 These Spanish oranges are delicios.
5 Our house is tipical of the villages around here.
6 We found the excercises very difficult.
7 He enjoys fisical activities like gardening.
8 Is there a diference in price between the two courses?

13 Correct the word order.
How is the station far?
How far is the station?
1 Is healthier life in the country?
2 So I think.
3 She always very carefully drives.
4 Is here your change.
5 The journey a lot of money costs.
6 Turn at the traffic lights left.

14 Correct the sentences.
How many water is there?
How much water is there?
1 We haven't got much apples.
2 I eat many fresh fruit.
3 A lot people go away at weekends.
4 She shouldn't to go. She's too young.
5 You've got a dog, no?
6 It takes the journey an hour.
7 I am not agree with you.
8 She isn't keen about junk food.
9 You spend all your money with clothes.

> At the end of the Progress Check, look back at your mistakes and study the Grammar Reference section for further help.

10 Describing things

Lost property

Focus

- Lost property
- Indefinite pronouns: *someone*, *anything*, etc.
- Indefinite adverbs of place: *everywhere*, etc.

1 Read the article about a Lost Property Office in central London and answer the questions.
1. What do you think 'the Number 17' is?
2. True or false? The office keeps property that people leave:
   a) on planes.
   b) on buses.
   c) in the street.
   d) on underground trains.
3. What's Maureen Beaumont's job?
4. What does she do if there's a name on the lost item?
5. What happens to the item if there's no name on it?
6. What reasons does Maureen give for liking her job?

2 Work with a partner and make a list of items that people often lose when they're travelling.

bags, …

3 🔊 Now listen to Maureen Beaumont talking about her job and answer the questions.
1. How many things come into the office on a normal day?
2. How many umbrellas come in on a rainy day?
3. How many umbrellas came in last year?

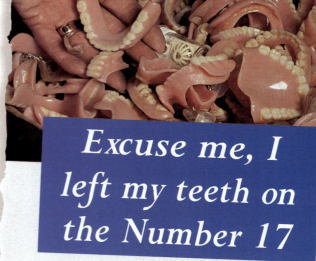

Excuse me, I left my teeth on the Number 17

If you leave something important on a bus or underground train while travelling around London, you should pay a visit to the London Transport Lost Property Office in central London.

'We've got everything here, but it's difficult to imagine how people lose some things,' says manager Maureen Beaumont, holding a box of false teeth. 'How can anyone leave their teeth on a bus?

'If there's a name and address somewhere on the item, we try to contact the owner and return it. Visitors to London are always surprised to get their property back. If we can't find the owner anywhere, we keep the item here for three months and hope that someone will come into the office to claim it. If no one collects the item in that time, we sell it.

'It's an interesting job. People lose some unusual things and they're always pleased when they come into the office and find them.'

4 🔊 Listen again. Which of these things does Ms Beaumont say she has got in the office? Compare her list with your list from Exercise 2.

handbags   purses   umbrellas   watches   clocks
cameras   jackets   books   musical instruments

UNIT TEN

DISCOVERING LANGUAGE

5 Find these words in the article. Do they refer to people, places or things?

something   everything   somewhere
anyone   no one

Now answer the questions.
1 Which of the words above is often used in a question?
2 Which word means the same as 'not ... anyone'?
3 Find the word *no one* in the article. It is the subject of a verb. Is that verb singular or plural?

6 Now complete the chart with these words:

anywhere   nothing   somewhere   anything
everything   nowhere   something   everywhere

PERSON	PLACE	THING
everyone	.....	.....
someone	.....	.....
anyone	.....	.....
no one	.....	.....

7 📼 Word stress. Listen to the words in the chart and mark the main stress on each word.

éveryone

Listen again and repeat.

8 Complete this paragraph with words from the chart in Exercise 6.

(1) ..... loses more things than I do. In fact, I lose (2) ..... almost every day. I leave umbrellas (3) ....., especially on buses, and I don't usually find them again. My mother says that she isn't going to lend me (4) ..... in future. Actually, I lost her car last week. I borrowed it to go to the cinema and when I came out, I couldn't find it (5) ...... Fortunately, I knew the registration number, and in the end (6) ..... found it for me in a completely different street!

9 Ask about the last time that your partner lost something. Ask these questions:
1 What did you lose?
2 Was it important?
3 Where did you look?
4 Did you find it?

10 The objects in the pictures below are also in the London Transport Lost Property Office. Match the pictures with these words and phrases. Use a dictionary to help you.

1 – *a sword*

a pair of handcuffs   a sword   part of a skeleton
a false hand   a wedding dress   an accordion

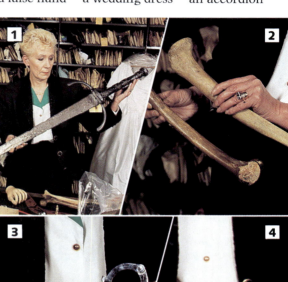

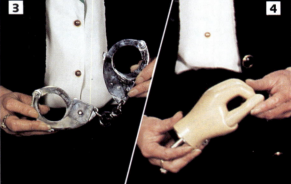

11 Work with a partner. Imagine that you lost one of the things above. Make up a story to explain how you lost it.

I'm an artist. I'm doing some drawings for a book on anatomy – for medical students. I borrowed the bones from a medical school and I left them on the bus.

73

Focus

- Objects
- Materials

- Describing things
- Talking about colour, size, weight and material
- Describing shape

- Questions:
  What colour?
  What shape?
  How big?
  How heavy?
- Present simple passive:
  be made of

Giving details

1 🔲 **Listen and read. Rosie Brady is talking to her brother, James, on the telephone. Describe Rosie's present to James. Can you guess what it is?**

ROSIE: I made your birthday present yesterday.
JAMES: You made it! What is it?
ROSIE: I'm not telling you. I'll bring it to London next week.
JAMES: OK. Let me guess. What colour is it?
ROSIE: Um ... it's green and blue.
JAMES: So what shape is it?
ROSIE: Rectangular, I suppose.
JAMES: Hmm. And, um, how big is it?
ROSIE: Oh, about 30 centimetres wide ... and ... 2 metres long.
JAMES: Really? How heavy is it?
ROSIE: I've got no idea. Less than a kilo.
JAMES: Right. And, um, what's it made of?
ROSIE: Wool.
JAMES: Oh, I know! It's a ...
ROSIE: See you next week, James. Bye!

2 🔲 **Stress and intonation. Listen and repeat.**

1 What <u>colour</u> is it?
2 What <u>shape</u> is it?
3 How <u>big</u> is it?
4 How <u>heavy</u> is it?
5 What's it <u>made</u> of?

3 Match the objects in the picture with these descriptions.

1 – D

1 It's square, it's made of plastic, and it's about 5 1/4 inches by 5 1/4 inches (about 13 centimetres by 13 centimetres).
2 It's round and 45 centimetres in diameter. It's made of glass, and the frame is made of wood.
3 It's about 2 metres (about 7 feet) high and it's made of metal.
4 It's made of soft black leather. It's 32 centimetres by 28 centimetres by 5 centimetres. It's rectangular, and it's got two leather handles and two side pockets.
5 The face is triangular and it's made of glass. The strap is made of metal.
6 It's oval and it's made of blue wool.

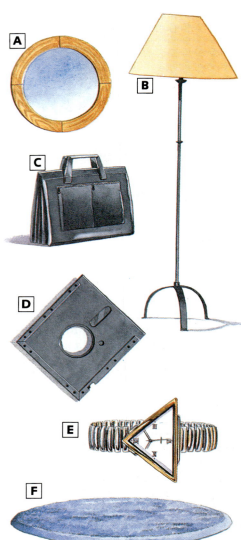

4 Say what shapes these are.

1 It's square.

5 Work in pairs.

Student A: Ask questions like the ones in Exercise 2 and identify the three objects in your partner's pictures. Then answer your partner's questions about the objects below.

Student B: Turn to page 121 and answer your partner's questions.

1 a frisbee

2 a pencil case

3 a wallet

6 Work in groups. One person thinks of an object. The other students in the group ask questions to find out what it is. The only question that you can't ask is: *What is it?*

COMPARING CULTURES

7 Is it common in your country to buy second-hand or used items? Say which of these things people buy second-hand and how they find them.

clothes   furniture   cars   bicycles and other vehicles

8 Work in pairs. Read this advertisement in a newsagent's for second-hand furniture and equipment.

Student A: Phone the number at the bottom of the advertisement. You want to buy all the items, but you want more information. Ask for the information and make notes.

B: 865412.
A: *Hello. I saw your advertisement at the newsagent's. Could you give me some information about the carpet?*
B: *Certainly. What would you like to know?*
A: …

Student B: You are selling the items. Turn to page 121 and answer your partner's questions.

Now change roles.

Student A: You are selling the items below.

```
FOR SALE                                    Tel 422307
Tent – £35
nylon, blue and green; 1m high, 120cm wide,
190 cm deep (for two people)
Portable CD player – £60
with radio, stereo headphones, case. No batteries.
16 cm x 13 cm x 6 cm. Weighs 2 kg.
3 shelves – £10 each
wood, black, 2m x 20 cm
```

FOR SALE

Large carpet £150
Colour TV £50
Computer desk £85

Telephone 865412

9 Use your notes from Exercise 8. Write sentences describing the items that you asked about. Then read your partner's sentences and correct any mistakes.

The carpet is rectangular. It's 4 metres by 6 metres. It's dark grey and it's made of nylon.

ENGLISH AROUND YOU

Paul Money Mark Hill Gene Abbott Josh Lofrano Mildred Cookson

Focus

- Clothes
- Materials

- Describing clothes
- Asking what something is like
- Talking about possessions

- Adjectives and order of adjectives
- Possessive pronouns: *mine, yours*, etc.

Describing clothes

1 🔊 Listen to these five people talking about their favourite sweaters. Match the sweaters with the people.

Gene Abbott – *Sweater 1*

2 Work with a partner and check your answers. Describe each sweater.

A: Whose is the first sweater? It's blue and it's made of wool.
B: It's Gene Abbott's.

DISCOVERING LANGUAGE

3 In Unit 4 you saw that adjectives of quality usually come before adjectives of colour. Look at these descriptions. What other rule can you make about the order of the adjectives?
1 It's a **large, blue, woollen** sweater.
2 My favourite sweater is a **small, red, cashmere** one.
3 I've got a **beautiful, green, leather** jacket.
4 I've got a lot of sandals, but I like wearing these **old, brown, plastic** ones when the weather is hot.
5 They're selling **cheap, white, cotton** T-shirts.

4 Now write descriptions of the sweaters in Exercise 1 in the same way.

5 Read the descriptions of two jackets and match the texts with the pictures. Then use a dictionary and label the pictures.

031 This is a light polyester jacket with long sleeves and a matching belt. There's a zip at the front and a hood for wet weather.

032 This is a warm woollen jacket with buttons down the front, side pockets and a top pocket. It is checked with a plain collar.

6 Ask and answer about favourite clothes.
A: Have you got a favourite jacket/pair of trousers?
B: Yes, I have.
A: What's it like?/What are they like?
B: It's .../They're ... It's got .../They've got ...

7 Write a description of a piece of clothing that one of your fellow students is wearing. Read it to the class. Other students will try to guess whose clothing you are describing. Follow the examples in Exercise 3.
They are blue denim jeans with ...

8 James and Julia are leaving a restaurant together. Look at the picture and say what they are wearing. Then listen to their conversation with the waiter. What's the problem?

DISCOVERING LANGUAGE

9 Listen to the conversation again. Replace the phrases in italics below with a word from the chart.
1 Er ... this isn't *my coat*.
2 What's *your coat* like?
3 *His coat* is a long black leather one.

my	your	his	her	our	their
mine	yours	his	hers	ours	theirs

Now make a rule about the different uses of *my/your*, etc. and *mine/yours*, etc.

10 Choose a word to complete the sentences.
1 Is this ..... scarf? Or is that one ..... ? (her/hers)
2 Those aren't ..... children. ..... are with friends. (ours/our)
3 I don't think that's .... suitcase is green. (their/theirs)

11 Work in pairs. Look at the coats below.
Student A: One of the coats is your partner's. Find out which one it is.
Student B: Choose a coat, but don't tell your partner. Answer questions about it.
A: Is this coat yours?
B: No, it isn't.
A: What's yours like?
B: Mine's a long, black, leather coat with a belt.
A: Yours is Coat 3.
B: Yes, that's right.

Development

BAGGAGE ENQUIRY

PERSONAL DETAILS
Surname .... Mr/Mrs/Miss/Ms
First name(s) ....
Address in the UK ....
....
Telephone number ....

FLIGHT DETAILS
Flight number ....
Arriving from ....
....

DESCRIPTION OF BAGGAGE
Give a full description of each bag (colour, size, material)
....
....
....

LISTENING AND WRITING

1 🖥 Maura Mattioli is returning to London from Italy. When she arrives at the airport, she can't find her baggage. Listen to her conversation with an airport official and complete the Baggage Enquiry form.

SPEAKING

2 Work in pairs.
Student A: You work at the Lost Luggage Office at an airport. Try to identify your partner's suitcase from the suitcases below. Ask about colour, size and material.
Student B: You are at an airport and can't find your suitcase. Turn to page 121.

1   2   3   4   5   6

READING

3 In 1895 Oscar Wilde wrote a play called *The Importance of Being Earnest*. Read this extract from it, but do not try to understand every word. Note these definitions and check other important words in your dictionary.

> **perambulator (pram)** a baby's bed on wheels for taking a baby outside
>
> **bassinette** the part of a pram that is a bed

Are these sentences true or false?
1 Miss Prism went out with the baby and a book.
2 Miss Prism lost the book.
3 She put the baby in her handbag.
4 She left the perambulator at a station.
5 The police found the perambulator.
6 Lady Bracknell found the baby.

NOTE: Lady Bracknell employed Miss Prism to look after her baby.

LADY BRACKNELL: ... Twenty-eight years ago, Prism, you left Lord Bracknell's house, Number 104, Upper Grosvenor Square, in charge of a perambulator that contained a baby of the male sex. You never returned. A few weeks later, through the elaborate investigations of the Metropolitan police, the perambulator was discovered at midnight standing by itself in a remote corner of Bayswater. It contained the manuscript of a three volume novel of more than usually revolting sentimentality ... But the baby was not there ... Prism! Where is that baby?

MISS PRISM: Lady Bracknell, I admit with shame that I do not know ... On the morning of the day you mention, a day that is forever branded on my memory, I prepared as usual to take the baby out in its perambulator. I had also with me a somewhat old, but capacious handbag in which I intended to place the manuscript of a work of fiction that I had written during my few unoccupied hours. In a moment of mental distraction, for which I can never forgive myself, I deposited the manuscript in the bassinette and placed the baby in the handbag.

JACK: ... But where did you deposit the handbag? ...

MISS PRISM: I left it in the cloakroom of one of the larger railway stations in London.

Summary

FUNCTIONS

Talking about dimensions
How big/long/wide is it?
It's 75 centimetres long/wide.

Talking about materials
What's it made of?
It's made of plastic.

Talking about possession
Whose is this?
It's mine.
Is this yours?
Yes, it is./No, it isn't.

Describing shape
What shape is it?
It's round./It's a round object.

Asking what something is like
What's yours like?

GRAMMAR

Questions with *how* + adjective
How big?   How wide?
How long? How heavy?

Present simple passive form (restricted use)
What's it made of?
It's made of metal and wood.

Possessive pronouns
mine   yours   his/hers/its
ours   theirs

Prepositional phrases
A black leather coat *with* a hood, a zip, etc.

Indefinite pronouns
someone   anyone   everyone   no one
something anything   everything   nothing

Indefinite adverbs of place
somewhere anywhere   everywhere   nowhere

Order of adjectives

	QUALITY	COLOUR	MATERIAL	
a	long	black	leather	coat

See the Grammar Reference section at the back of the book for more information.

11 You and your body

The human body

Focus

- Parts of the body
- Aches and pains

- Asking about problems
- Talking about illness
- Making suggestions
- Giving advice: *Why don't you...?/You should(n't)...*

- Further practice: *have/has got*

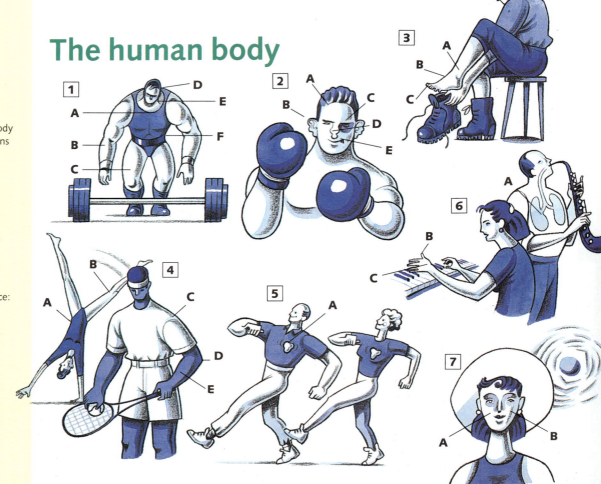

1 Look at the pictures showing parts of the human body. Label the parts that you know and use these clues to label the rest. Then check with a dictionary.

1 Lifting weights builds up the muscles in your *arms*, *chest* and *neck*. It's important to lift correctly. If you don't bend your *legs*, you can hurt your *back*. You should never bend your body at the *waist*.
2 Boxers, of course, suffer from *head* injuries – a broken *nose*, a black *eye*, a cut *mouth* or a swollen *ear* is common.
3 People who climb mountains have to wear good, heavy shoes or boots to protect their *feet* and *toes*. Boots usually have high sides to support the *ankles*.
4 Gymnasts often have problems with their *hips* and *knees*; tennis players have more problems with their *arms*, especially their *elbows* and *shoulders*.
5 Daily exercise is good for you. It helps to prevent *heart* attacks in middle-aged people.
6 Pianists often have strong, sensitive *hands* and long *fingers*. If you play a wind instrument like the saxophone, you need good *lungs*.
7 In strong sun, most people with white *skin* need a hat to protect their head and *face* and strong cream on the rest of their body.

2 Name the parts of the body.

You need to know these sizes when you buy a man's shirt. – neck/chest

1 You need to know these sizes when you buy jeans or trousers.
2 You play the guitar with them.
3 The place where your leg bends.
4 The place where your arm bends.
5 The parts of your body that you use for:
   a) eating   c) seeing
   b) hearing   d) breathing

3 Say which parts of the body are most important to the people below and why.

The most important part(s) of the body for a ... is/are ...

1 a painter   3 a pilot   5 a Sumo wrestler
2 a runner   4 a drummer   6 a swimmer

4 Listen and read. Tom Hall's son, Bob, is moving out of his parents' house into a flat. Penny, his girlfriend, is helping him. Answer the questions.

1 What's wrong with Bob?
2 What's Penny's advice to him?

BOB: Oh!
PENNY: Bob? What's the matter?
BOB: My arms hurt.
PENNY: I'm not surprised. Why don't you stop for a moment? Let's have a cup of tea!
BOB: That's a good idea. I think I will.
PENNY: You should ask me to help you with the heavier boxes.
BOB: Yes. You're probably right. Er, where did we put the tea?

DISCOVERING LANGUAGE

5 Read the conversation again. Find two ways of giving advice.

6 Work with a partner. Make conversations for the situations below. Use some of the suggestions or your own ideas.

A: What's the matter?
B: My ... hurts/hurt.
A: Why don't you ... ?/You should ...
B: That's a good idea. I think I will.

> SUGGESTIONS
>
> rest   go to bed   stop work/eating   lie/sit down
> put some cream/a plaster on   stay at home
> go to the dentist/doctor   keep warm
> take an aspirin/some medicine

7 Ask and answer about the situations below. Use the suggestions from Exercise 6 to help you.

A: What's the matter with him?/What's wrong with him?
B: He's got a headache.
A: He should take an aspirin.

1 a headache   2 a cold   3 coughs

4 toothache   5 earache   6 stomachache

8 Stress and intonation. Listen and repeat. Underline the main stress in each sentence.

He's got a <u>head</u>ache.

1 She's got a cold.   4 He's got earache.
2 They've got coughs.   5 She's got stomachache.
3 She's got toothache.

Focus

- Accidents
- Talking about events in the recent past
- Present perfect simple: *have/has* + past participle
- Adverb: *just*

Accidents

1 Look at Marco's room above. A friend is bringing her small children to visit him. Make a list of things that he should do before they come.

clear the table, ...

2 🔲 Listen to a telephone conversation between Marco and Teresa. Tick the things on your list from Exercise 1 that Marco has done.

TERESA: Hi, Marco. What are you doing?
MARCO: I'm tidying my room. Jean and her kids are coming round. Have you seen those children? They're little monsters.
TERESA: They're sweet! But Marco, you should sort out your room before they arrive. Your fire's not safe for children.
MARCO: I know. It's all right. I've bought a fireguard.
TERESA: And have you moved your records and CDs?
MARCO: No, I haven't, but I'm going to put them under the bed.
TERESA: What about all those glasses? What have you done with them?
MARCO: I've put them on a higher shelf. And I've locked all the cupboards. Er, have you had coffee?
TERESA: Yes, I have – and no, I don't want to come and help. See you later, Marco!
MARCO: Bye, Teresa.

3 🔲 Stress and intonation. Listen to this part of the conversation again. Underline the stressed words.

MARCO: They're little monsters.
TERESA: They're sweet!

Now read these conversations in pairs. Stress the contrasted words.

A: *It's warm today, isn't it.*
B: *What? It's freezing!*

A: *Let's go. It's late.*
B: *What do you mean? It's still early.*

🔲 Listen and check your pronunciation.

DISCOVERING LANGUAGE

4 The present perfect simple is formed with *have/has* + past participle. Read the conversation in Exercise 2 again. Find examples of the present perfect simple and choose the best ending to this statement.

The present perfect is often used to refer to events:
a) that happened at a particular, specified time in the past.
b) that are happening now.
c) that happened at an unspecified time in the recent past.

5 Look again at the forms of the past participle in Exercise 2, and complete the chart.

INFINITIVE	PAST SIMPLE	PAST PARTICIPLE
see	saw	seen
buy	bought	.....
move	moved	.....
do	did	.....
put	put	.....
lock	locked	.....
have	had	.....

6 Which two verbs in the chart are regular verbs? How is the past participle of regular verbs formed?

7 Ask and answer about the people in the pictures below. Use the pronouns and the verb chart below to help you.

Picture 1
A: *What's she done?*
B: *She's fallen down the stairs.*

INFINITIVE	PAST PARTICIPLE
fall	fallen
cut	cut
hit	hit
burn	burnt
eat	eaten
break	broken
smash	smashed

1 she

2 he

3 she

4 they

5 she

6 you/I

7 you/we

8 Read this dialogue. Which word tells you that something happened a very short time ago? Notice the position of the word in the sentence.

A: *Your hair's wet. Is it raining?*
B: *No, I've just washed it.*

Now write sentences about the people in Exercise 7.

1 *The woman has just fallen down the stairs.*

9 Use the regular verbs below and ask your partner about things he/she has done today.

A: *Have you washed your face?*
B: *Yes, I have./No, I haven't.*

wash	watch
cook	clean
phone	play
tidy	listen

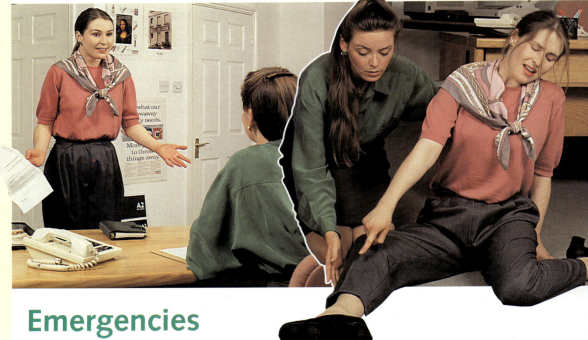

Focus

- Emergency procedures
- Body language

- Further practice: giving advice

- Further practice: present perfect simple

- Further practice: modal: *should* + infinitive

Emergencies

1 Look at the pictures of Rachel above. Say what you think has just happened and what is happening now in each picture.

2 📺 Listen to the conversation between Rachel, Julia and Tom at MAP Advertising. Answer the questions.
1. What has Rachel won?
2. Has she broken her leg?
3. What does Tom think she should do?
4. What do you think is going to happen next?

↻ COMPARING CULTURES

3 Read the information from a telephone directory about British emergency services. Imagine what Tom did when Rachel had her accident. Answer the questions.
1. What number did Tom phone?
2. Who did he speak to first?
3. What information did he give?
4. Who did he speak to next?
5. What information did he give?

4 What happens in your country? What number do you dial in an emergency? What information do you give? Tell your partner if you have been in this situation in the past.

999 EMERGENCY
SOS Emergency calls

Dial 999.

Tell the telephone operator which service you want.

Give your telephone number.

Wait for the emergency service operator to answer.

Give the address where help is needed.

Give any other important information.

Fire Police Ambulance Coastguard Mountain rescue Cave rescue

Tom Hall
MANAGING DIRECTOR

Marketing
Advertising
Publicity

42 Kingsway,
London WC2 4BB
tel: 071 636 2091
fax: 071 240 7722

Body language

COMPARING CULTURES

1 We communicate with words, but also with our bodies. At least one person in each of the pictures below is feeling uncomfortable for some reason. Match the thoughts below with the people. Then say what the other people in each picture are thinking.

1–F Oh, they've arrived at last! Why couldn't they arrive on time!

1 Oh dear! We're late! How embarrassing. They've started eating.
2 Why is he touching me like this?
3 Why is he bowing to me? Should I bow too?
4 Oh no! My clothes are too casual!
5 Why is he standing so near me? When I take a step back, he takes a step closer!
6 I don't trust this man. He isn't looking me in the eye.

2 Work with a partner. Discuss how true the statements below are in your country. Write new statements for any sentences which are not true.

You should always arrive on time, especially for business appointments.
This is generally true in my country, but if people invite you to their home, it is usual to arrive five or ten minutes late.

1 It is important to wear the right kind of clothes.
2 You should look at people's eyes frequently when they talk to you. If you don't, you seem uncomfortable or unfriendly.
3 You should stand about a metre away from someone. If you are good friends you can stand closer, about half a metre away.
4 You shouldn't touch someone for more than a few seconds if you do not know them very well. They will feel uncomfortable.
5 You should be careful about the gestures that you make to foreigners. An innocent gesture in one country may be offensive in another.

Development

LISTENING

1 🔊 Listen to Mary Evelyn, from the London Contemporary Dance School. List the parts of the body that she talks about.

arms, ...

2 🔊 Listen again. Choose the correct answer according to what Mary Evelyn says.
1. Now she is:
   a) a professional dancer.
   b) a dance teacher.
2. Dancers use ..... to tell stories.
   a) words
   b) their bodies
3. Dancers ..... strong.
   a) have to be
   b) don't have to be
4. Good dancers can move each part of their body ..... the other parts.
   a) at the same time as
   b) separately from

THE PLACE
The Place is internationally known as the home of London Contemporary Dance School (LCDS) and The Place Theatre. The Evening School has been part of LCDS for over twenty years and provides tuition of the highest quality.

CONTEMPORARY DANCE
Level 1 A class for complete beginners.
Level 2 A basic level class for students with some experience.
Level 3A For students with a good knowledge of contemporary or classical dance.
Level 3B For students with at least one year's experience. Minimum attendance of two classes a week.
Level 4 A highly technical class for those with confidence and proficiency in contemporary dance.

CLASSICAL BALLET
Basic Suitable for contemporary dance students at Level 2 and for those with a small amount of experience in classical dance.
Intermediate Suitable for contemporary dance students at Levels 3A, 3B and 4 and for those with good experience of classical dance.

JAZZ
For anyone except complete beginners.

BODY CONDITIONING
For dancers and non-dancers. No experience needed.

READING

3 The London Contemporary Dance School has an evening school for members of the public. Read the brochure above and answer the questions.
1. Which of the following can you do at the evening school?
   a) ballet   c) jazz dancing
   b) disco dancing d) drama
2. How much does it cost for a single class?
3. How much does it cost to do a Level 1 class once a week for the autumn term?

SPEAKING

4 Work in pairs.
Student A: You work at the evening school. Give your partner the information he/she wants about the classes available.
Student B: You want to do some classes in the evening. Turn to page 122.

TIMETABLE

Monday	6.30–8.00 p.m.	Level 2 / Level 3A / Intermediate Ballet / Professional Class
Tuesday	6.30–8.00 p.m.	Level 1 / Level 2 / Level 3B / Level 4
Wednesday	6.30–8.00 p.m.	Level 1 / Level 3B / Basic Ballet / Professional Class
Thursday	6.30–8.00 p.m.	Level 3B / Level 4 / Body Conditioning / Level 3A
Friday	6.30–8.00 p.m.	Jazz / Professional Class
Saturday	6.30–7.30 p.m. / 10.00–11.30 a.m.	Level 3A / Level 1

TERM DATES
Term 1: 16 September–7 December (12 weeks)
Term 2: 6 January–28 March (12 weeks)
Term 3: 27 April–11 July (11 weeks)

FEES
Single class rate Available for all levels. £4.20.
Professional class available at single class rate only.
Per Term For all levels except the professional classes.

	Terms 1 and 2 (autumn and spring)	Term 3 (summer)
1 class per week	£49	£45
2 classes per week	£97	£89
3 classes per week	£144	£133
4 classes per week	£190	£175
5 classes per week	£231	£214

READING AND WRITING

5 Read the text below about a principal dancer in a ballet company. Then rewrite the text to include the extra information in the notes below.

Viviana works for the Royal Ballet Company in London. She came to Britain as a child and studied at the Royal Ballet School. She could not speak English and she missed her family a lot, but she was already a very good dancer. In 1984 she joined the Royal Ballet. A few years later a soloist in *Swan Lake* hurt herself in the second act and Viviana had to take her part. Soon after that, she became a principal dancer.

BIOGRAPHICAL NOTES
NAME: Viviana Durante
PHYSICAL APPEARANCE: small and strong; long neck, pale skin, dark hair and eyes.
YEAR OF BIRTH: 1968
PLACE OF BIRTH: Rome
NATIONALITY: Italian
MOVED TO BRITAIN: 1978
OCCUPATION: Dancer (became principal 1989)

UNIT ELEVEN

Summary

FUNCTIONAL LANGUAGE

Asking about problems
What's the matter?
What's wrong with you?

Talking about illness
I've got a headache.

Talking about events in the recent past
She's hurt her leg.
I've just washed my hair.

Giving advice
You should take some aspirin.
You shouldn't carry heavy boxes.

Making suggestions
Why don't you have a cup of tea?

GRAMMAR

The present perfect simple
have/has + past participle
(*-ed* for regular verbs)
AFFIRMATIVE
I/you/we/they have seen a mouse.
He/she/it has seen a mouse.
NEGATIVE
I/you/we/they haven't seen a mouse.
He/she/it hasn't seen a mouse.
INTERROGATIVE AND SHORT ANSWERS
Have I/you/we/they seen a mouse?
Yes, I/you/we/they have.
No, I/you/we/they haven't.
Has he/she/it seen a mouse?
Yes, he/she/it has.
No, he/she/it hasn't.
ADVERB
just

See the Grammar Reference section at the back of the book for more information.

12 People's lives

Achievements

Focus

- Individual achievements
- Describing people and jobs
- Talking about past experiences
- Adverbs: *ever*, *never*
- Further practice: present perfect simple, superlative adjectives

1 Read the texts below. Explain why each person is famous.

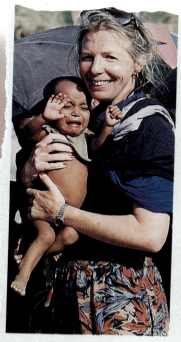

Sigeru Miyamoto works for the Japanese company Nintendo. In 1983, when he was thirty-two, he created Super Mario Brothers. This became the most successful video game in the world, with annual sales of $4.3 billion. 'I knew the game would sell, but I've never understood why it is so popular,' says Mr Miyamoto. With the help of Super Mario, the Nintendo Entertainment System has become one of the best-selling toys in history.

When Pat Kerr was a stewardess with British Airways, she flew regularly between Britain and Bangladesh. Between flights she spent her time with children in a Dhaka orphanage, and she began to feel that she wanted to do more to help. 'Have you ever seen the faces of children without hope … without a future?' she asks her interviewer. 'I had no choice.'

She gave up her job to work in Bangladesh full time, and she raised almost a million pounds to build a new orphanage. There children get food, clothes, classes in Bengali and English, and work training. 'I've never felt so useful in all my life,' Ms Kerr says. 'I know I'm doing the right thing.'

Ocsi Tabak comes from a Hungarian circus family. He is one of Europe's last human cannonballs. On most nights since he was twelve, he has flown through the air at 90 kilometres an hour into a net. Now he wants to try the stunt with a bag over his head. He has also ordered a special cannon so that he and his son can fly together – he has never tried a double act before.

  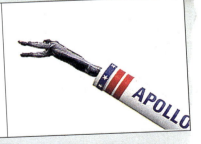

2 Answer the questions about the texts.
1 Who:
   a) works with children?
   b) does dangerous stunts?
   c) works with computer systems?
2 What is *Super Mario Brothers*?
3 Where does Pat Kerr work?
4 When did Ocsi Tabak become a human cannonball?

3 Work with a partner. Choose adjectives from the lists below to describe the people and jobs in Exercise 1. Use a dictionary to help you.

PERSON
brave clever kind successful

JOB
dangerous frightening difficult easy

PERSON OR JOB
boring important crazy interesting unusual ordinary

I think Sigeru Miyamoto has a very interesting job, and he is also very successful. He probably earns a lot of money.

DISCOVERING LANGUAGE

4 Look at the texts again. Find a sentence with the word *ever* and another with the word *never*. Then answer the questions.
1 What is the tense of the verb in each sentence?
2 Which sentence is:
   a) a statement?   b) a question?
3 Where do the words *ever* and *never* come in the sentences?

Now check with these sentences. Are your answers the same?

Have you ever been to the circus?
Have you ever played a video game?
I've never seen a human cannonball.
They have never known their parents.

5 🔊 Stress and intonation. Listen to these sentences. Underline the main stresses. Then listen again and repeat.

Have you <u>ev</u>er been to the <u>cir</u>cus?
1 Have they ever had a computer?
2 Has he ever travelled by plane?
3 I've never seen that stunt.
4 They've never had computer games.
5 He's never been abroad.

6 Think of all the things that you have never done and that you want to do. Complete the questionnaire.

		REASON
A place to visit	Egypt	to see the Pyramids
A way of travelling	.....	.....
Something to see	.....	.....
Something to do	.....	.....
A sport to try	.....	.....
Something to eat	.....	.....
Something to drink	.....	.....
A person to meet	.....	.....

Now ask about your partner's answers.
A: I've never been to Egypt.
B: Why do you want to go there?
A: Because I'd like to see the pyramids.

7 Write about your partner's answers to Exercise 6 and tell the class.

Emma has never been to Egypt. She wants to go there because she'd like to see the Pyramids.

8 Read this conversation. Say how the main tense changes.
A: Have you ever had an embarrassing experience?
B: Yes, I have.
A: What's the most embarrassing experience that you've ever had?
B: I invited a friend to a meal in an expensive restaurant and I left all my money at home.

Complete the chart below to show the structure of the second question. Then ask your partner the same question.

QUESTION WORD	VERB *BE*	ARTICLE	SUPERLATIVE ADJECTIVE	NOUN
What	's	.....	.....	.....

(that)

NOUN / PRONOUN	HAS / HAVE		PAST PARTICIPLE
.....	.....	ever	..... ?

9 Now use the prompts to ask your partner similar questions.
1 have/bad holiday?
2 lose/important papers?
3 meet/famous person?
4 eat/unusual food?
5 stay/beautiful place?

Focus

- Life changes
- Periods of time
- Talking about situations that continue into the present
- Expressing regret
- Apologising

- Adverbs: *for, since*
- Further practice: present perfect simple

Changes

1 🔲 **Alan is visiting Rosie's flat. Listen to their conversation. Are these statements true or false?**

1 Alan wants to leave his job.
2 He wants to leave Brighton.
3 He wants to live in London.
4 He doesn't want to see Rosie again.
5 He has made a sudden decision.

2 🔲 **Listen again and read. Complete the conversation.**

ALAN: Rosie, I've got something to tell you.
ROSIE: What is it?
ALAN: Well, I've made a decision. I'm going to leave the hospital.
ROSIE: Leave? What do you mean?
ALAN: I'm bored with it. I want to do something different.
ROSIE: I see. (1) ..... have you been at the hospital? For two years?
ALAN: No, I've been there (2) ....., and I've been in Brighton (3) ...... I want a change.
ROSIE: You're leaving *Brighton*! But why? What are you going to do?
ALAN: I'm going to Africa. I've got a job as a nurse with a voluntary organisation. They want me to go to Nigeria.
ROSIE: What! You're joking!
ALAN: Look, I didn't tell you before because nothing was certain. But I got a letter this morning. Rosie, I'm going to miss you very much, and I don't want our relationship to end. But I want to see the world. You do understand, don't you?
ROSIE: Oh, yes, I understand!
ALAN: I'm really sorry, Rosie.

DISCOVERING LANGUAGE

3 Look at the phrases that you added to the conversation in Exercise 2 and answer the questions.

1 Is Alan working at the hospital now?
2 How long has he worked there?
3 When did he move to Brighton?
4 Is he living there now?
5 How long has he lived there?

4 Work in pairs. Read the sentences and discuss the different uses of *for* and *since* to describe periods of time.

1 Alan and Rosie have been friends for nine months.
2 Rosie has worked in Brighton for a year.
3 Rosie has lived in Britain since 1992.
4 Alan has thought about leaving since last November.

5 Complete these sentences with *for* or *since*.

1 She's had that bag ..... three months, I think.
2 I've been a secretary ..... 1989.
3 They've lived in the area ..... last March.
4 We've known them ..... years and years.
5 He's learnt English ..... he was twelve.
6 You've played the guitar ..... a long time, haven't you?

6 Group the time expressions below into:
1 expressions that follow *for*:
a long time
2 expressions that follow *since*:
I was a child

… a long time   … I was a child   … months
… ages   … I was a teenager   … last summer
… years   … the beginning of the year
… I started school

7 Now make affirmative and negative sentences which are true about yourself. Use the expressions from Exercise 6.
I haven't seen my grandmother for a long time.
I've lived in this town since I was a child.

8 Work in pairs. Ask your partner questions beginning *How long*. Use these verbs:
have   be   live   know   learn   play
A: *How long have you had that coat?*
B: *I've had it for two or three years.*

9 Like Alan, Julia has made a decision. Listen to her conversation with Tom Hall and answer the questions.
1 What is her decision?
2 Has she enjoyed working at MAP Advertising?
3 How long has she worked there?
4 What are the reasons for her decision?
5 What is Tom's reaction?

10 Stress and intonation. Listen again to Tom. Which words does he stress?
I'm really sorry …

Practise the phrase. Then listen and repeat these other ways of expressing regret.
I'm so sorry.   I'm very sorry.   I'm terribly sorry.
I'm awfully sorry.

COMPARING CULTURES

11 *Sorry* is also used when we:
1 interrupt another speaker.
2 ask someone to repeat something.
3 bump into someone in the street.
4 tell someone politely that they have made a mistake.
5 correct something we said earlier.

Match the pictures below with the uses of *sorry* above.
1 – C

12 What do you say in the same situations in your language? Are there other situations when you say sorry?

Development

SPEAKING

1 Work with a partner. Discuss why some people live for a long time and others do not. Consider these possible factors:

work   leisure   money   diet   friends   family

READING

2 Read the article about Charlotte Hughes. Say why she thinks she has had a long life.

3 Answer the questions.
1 How old is Mrs Hughes?
2 What changes has she seen in her lifetime?
3 Where does she live now?
4 How old was she when she started work?
5 What was her job?
6 How old was she when she got married?
7 What did her husband do?
8 What does the Queen do when British people celebrate their 100th birthday?

4 Find a word or phrase in the article that means:
1 a type of officer in the army.
2 a vehicle pulled by horses.
3 an old-fashioned machine for playing records.
4 the political leader of Britain (and many other countries).
5 a home for people who need care and medical attention.

WRITING

5 Write about the life of an older person that you know. Write three paragraphs.

PARAGRAPH 1   A short biography.
PARAGRAPH 2   Changes during his/her lifetime.
PARAGRAPH 3   Reasons for a long life.

Twenty-two prime ministers have come and gone . . .

CHARLOTTE HUGHES was born in England on August 2nd 1877, the day Alexander Graham Bell started his first telephone company. She has travelled by horse-drawn carriage and Concorde, and seen the birth of the phonograph, the fax machine and the first test-tube baby.

'Healthy eating has a lot to do with living a long and honest life,' she said yesterday at the nursing home where she lives in Redcar, Cleveland, as she tucked into a breakfast of bacon and eggs.

Hughes spent her working years from the age of thirteen as a teacher. She did not marry until sixty-three. 'You were not allowed to teach and marry,' she explained on her last birthday. 'Teaching was the best paid job and I had no intention of giving it up.' Her husband was an army captain and they were together for forty years before he died at 103.

Hughes has watched the passing of twenty-two prime ministers. She is believed to be the second oldest person in the world, two years younger than Jeanne Louise Calment, a French woman. Calment only recently gave up cigarettes, but still enjoys chocolate.

Hughes believes she has had a long life because of her strong moral code. She is worried about the values of people today. Surrounded by cards and framed telegrams, she anticipates seeing at least one more Olympic games and receiving many more royal greetings. She said: 'Hopefully there will be a lot more messages from the Queen yet, as I think I will go on to be at least 120.'

LISTENING

6 🔊 Before Alan got his job in Nigeria, he had an interview. Listen to part of the interview and complete Alan's curriculum vitae (CV) and the interviewer's notes below.

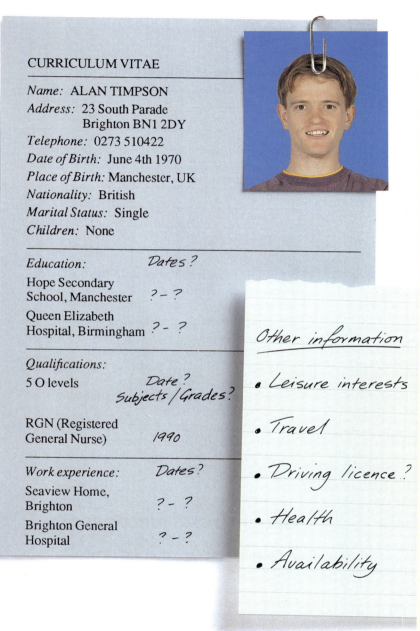

WRITING

7 Write a CV for yourself. Use the same format as the one above.

SPEAKING

8 Interview your partner and write his/her CV. Ask for other information that interests you.

Summary

FUNCTIONAL LANGUAGE

Asking about experiences
Have you ever had an accident?
Yes, I have./No I haven't.

Expressing regret
I'm so/very/really/terribly/ awfully sorry.

Interrupting
Sorry, ...

Asking for repetition
Sorry?

Correcting yourself
Sorry. ...

GRAMMAR

Present perfect simple + *for/since*
I've lived here for two years.
[*for* + period of time]
She's had that book since Saturday.
[*since* + point in time]

Past simple/present perfect
I moved here last year.
I've lived here for two years.
[I live here now.]

Present perfect simple + *ever/never*
Have you ever been to Egypt?
I've never been to Egypt.

Superlative adjective + present perfect
It's the best film I've ever seen.

See the Grammar Reference section at the back of the book for more information.

UNITS 10–12

Progress check 4

Vocabulary

1 Reorder the letters to make the names of materials.
dowo – *wood*
1 ltspiac   3 olwo   5 ltmae
2 lgsas   4 erealht 6 rapep

2 Draw the shapes.
It's square.
1 It's triangular.   3 It's round.
2 It's rectangular.   4 It's oval.

3 Label the picture with these words.
belt zip collar sleeve
button hood pocket
1 – *belt*

4 Look at the picture and put the parts of the body below into three groups.

A	B	C
head		

arm leg foot chest
waist toe knee nose
mouth ankle elbow
heart lung brain
shoulder face head
finger

5 Find five more health problems in the box.

a	x	h	e	a	d	a	c	h	e	r	t
l	o	j	k	b	i	t	o	u	a	s	d
n	b	a	i	n	p	r	u	l	r	q	a
e	e	c	z	w	u	n	g	d	a	r	c
t	o	o	t	h	a	c	h	e	c	g	h
t	h	l	a	s	e	f	r	t	h	o	o
r	e	d	e	a	l	k	i	g	e	s	t
o	s	t	o	m	a	c	h	a	c	h	e

6 Complete each sentence with the best adjective from this list.

favourite bored clever ordinary
interesting useful frightening sensitive

1 This book's very .... I can't stop reading it.
2 Walking along dark streets at night is ....
3 He is a ...... child. He is always top of the class.
4 I was so ...... that I fell asleep.
5 She's just an ...... woman doing a normal job – but she's special to me.
6 Be careful how you tell him – he's very ....
7 It's my ...... magazine. It's excellent.
8 Can't you do something ...... like tidying your room?

Grammar and functions

7 Complete the sentences with a word beginning with *some-, any-, every-,* or *no-*.
I looked for my watch ....
I looked for my watch everywhere.
1 I couldn't find a parking place ....
2 ...... enjoys having a holiday.
3 Let's go ...... warm this year.
4 ...... likes me; I haven't got any true friends.
5 Have you got ...... to eat?
6 No, sorry. There's ...... in the fridge.
7 I saw ...... in the garden last night. He was definitely a stranger.

8 Write questions for the answers.

It's round.
What shape is it?
1 They're green.
2 It's about 2 metres long.
3 It's about 45 centimetres wide.
4 About 10 kilograms.
5 Metal and wood.
6 They're small, round and made of thin plastic.
7 It's Jim's.
8 Her back hurts.
9 China? No, we haven't.

9 Complete the pairs of sentences with the correct words.

1 That's not .... scarf is black. (my/mine)
2 Is that ..... cat? I thought ..... was black and white. (your/yours)
3 That definitely isn't ..... house. I think ..... is number seventeen. (their/theirs)
4 This cheque book is ..... . Look, ... name's on the cheques. (her/hers)
5 The jobs on this piece of paper are .... tasks are on this list here. (their/mine)
6 Where are ..... seats? ..... are at the back. (your/ours)

10 Write the past participles of these verbs.

become – *become*

become	.....	listen	.....
buy	.....	lock	.....
cut	.....	lose	.....
do	.....	make	.....
eat	.....	meet	.....
fall	.....	move	.....
feel	.....	put	.....
fly	.....	see	.....
have	.....	tidy	.....
hit	.....	try	.....
learn	.....	wash	.....

11 Write sentences. Say what each person has just done.

He has just phoned the police.

1 he's

2 she's

3 we've

4 you've

5 they've

6 I've

12 Complete the sentences with *for* or *since*.

1 I've lived in Glasgow ..... I was born.
2 They've worked here ..... years.
3 She's been married ..... a long time.
4 My brother has been in Japan ..... the last six months.
5 I've had a good time ..... my exams.
6 He's taught English ..... he left college.

Common errors

13 Correct the mistakes.

I've lost a teeth, but the dentist is going to put in a new one.
I've lost a tooth, ...
1 Can you give me an information about train times, please?
2 She's got terrible headache.
3 He's a doctor and it's a very hard work.
4 Please tidy all the cupboard.
5 It's most expensive holiday we've ever had.
6 I'm trying to lose weight, but I still love the chocolate.

14 Say which consonant in each word you do not pronounce when you speak.

honestly – *h*
1 listen   2 sword   3 ballet   4 when   5 vehicle

> At the end of the Progress Check, look back at your mistakes and study the Grammar Reference section for further help.

13 Things going wrong

Focus

- Accidents and disasters
- Reporting what someone said
- Further practice: talking about past experiences
- Present perfect/past simple contrast
- Reported statements
- Adverb: *ago*

Damage and loss

FLOODS HIT BANGLADESH
Thousands homeless

1 🔊 **Listen and read. Becky is reading a newspaper, and talking to Marco. Answer the questions.**
1 When was Marco in a flood?
2 Why did he have to leave his house?

BECKY: Oh, more floods in Bangladesh – those poor people! Have you ever been in a flood, Marco?
MARCO: Yes, I have.
BECKY: When was that?
MARCO: There was a terrible flood two years ago, when I lived in Venice.
BECKY: What happened?
MARCO: Well, it rained for about a week and then there was a storm. The water came up over the doorway of our house and filled the ground floor. It was about a metre deep. We had to leave the house for a month until it was dry again.

DISCOVERING LANGUAGE

2 Look again at the conversation in Exercise 1 and answer the questions.
1 Which tense is used for each question? Why does the tense change?
2 What year is it now? So what was the date two years ago?
3 Which tense is used with *ago*?

3 Now write true sentences about yourself using these expressions:
1 three years ago
My family moved to Rio three years ago./ Three years ago my family moved to Rio.
2 ten years ago   4 six months ago
3 a year ago   5 two weeks ago

4 Look at the pictures below. Talk about your own or your friends' experiences. Use these phrases:
be in a flood/a fire/a storm
have an accident/a break-in

A: Have you ever … ?
B: Yes, I have./No, I haven't, but my friend has.
A: When was that?
B: …
A: What happened?
B: …

1

2

3

4

5 🔊 Tom Hall is in his office waiting for a meeting with James and Julia. Listen and answer the questions.
1. Where has Julia been?
2. Why is she late?
3. What was in her briefcase?
4. When did she notice that she didn't have it?
5. Which picture shows what really happened?

6 Read these sentences from Tom's conversation with Julia. What did the people actually say?
1. They said the briefcase wasn't there.
   They said, '.....'
2. He said the papers had the name MAP on them.
   He said, '.....'

7 Work in pairs. Recreate Tom and Julia's conversation in Exercise 5.
Student A: You are Tom. Ask Julia where she has been and what happened.
Student B: You are Julia. Explain what happened. Use the notes below to help you.

a.m. with client – lunch with client – shopping – no cheque book – no briefcase – not in car – phoned client – not in client's office – police station

DISCOVERING LANGUAGE

8 Look at what people said, and how Julia and Tom report what they said. Then answer the questions.
a) CLIENT: 'Your briefcase isn't here.'
   JULIA: 'They said (that) my briefcase wasn't there.'
b) MANAGER: 'The papers have the name MAP on them.'
   TOM: 'He said (that) the papers had the name MAP on them.'
c) MANAGER: 'You can collect it any time.'
   JULIA: 'He said (that) I could collect it any time.'

1. How does the present tense verb change when the reporting verb (*say*) is in the past tense (*said*)?
2. Which word can follow the reporting verb?
3. How does the adverb *here* change when it is reported?
4. What other change do you notice in a)?

9 Report what Julia said to the shop assistant when she couldn't find her cheque book.
Julia said (that) . . .

❝ I'm sorry, but I can't find my cheque book. It isn't in my bag. I keep it in my briefcase, and I think that's in the car. ❞

DISCOVERING LANGUAGE

10 Look at these pairs of sentences. Each pair has the same meaning, but what is the difference between the two constructions?
1. They said (that) the bag wasn't there.
   They told me (that) the bag wasn't there.
2. He said (that) they had the name MAP on them.
   He told me (that) they had the name MAP on them.

11 James phoned Tom to say why <u>he</u> was late. Report what James said in these two ways:
'I'm at a garage.'
James said he was at a garage.
James told Tom he was at a garage.
1. 'There's a problem with my car.'
2. 'The brakes don't work.'
3. 'I can't drive it.'
4. 'I need a taxi.'

Asking for help

Focus
- Emergency and counselling services
- Problems and solutions
- Reporting what someone asked
- Reassuring and calming someone
- Reported questions
- Ask + if/what/how, etc.
- Further practice: reported speech

COMPARING CULTURES

1 Match the problems, 1–7, with the people or services, a)–g). Make sentences like the example.

If you have a fire, you call the fire brigade.

1 have/fire	a) the police
2 have/break-in	b) the fire brigade
3 lose/wallet	c) the ambulance service
4 be/ill	d) a solicitor
5 have/accident	e) a friend
6 have/legal problem	f) a doctor
7 have/emotional problem	g) the Lost Property Office

2 Which other people or organisations in your country give help and advice about particular problems?

3 Work with a partner. List problems that college students sometimes have when they live a long way from their families. Use a dictionary to help you.

4 Jan Murray is a student counsellor at a university in Britain. Read about her work and compare your list with the problems that she mentions.

DISCOVERING LANGUAGE

5 Look at the article again and find six reported questions that follow the verb *asked*. Write each one as a direct question.
1 Compare the direct and the reported questions. What is the position of the subject and verb in each case?
2 When is the word *if* used in reported questions?

6 Now report these questions.

Do I have to leave my room in the holidays?
Sue asked Jan if she had to leave her room in the holidays.

1 How can I get a room at the university?
   John asked her . . .
2 Is the medical centre open in the holidays?
   Bob and Kate asked her . . .
3 Can I talk to you about something personal?
   Marion asked her . . .
4 When is the office open in the evening?
   Sam asked her . . .

MY DAY...
JAN MURRAY · STUDENT COUNSELLOR

Jan Murray works at a university as a student counsellor. Students can come and see her if they need help or advice. I asked her when her office was open and what sort of problems students had.

'I'm here every day during the week, and my colleague is here in the evenings and at weekends. There's also an emergency telephone number at night.

'People come to me with all kinds of problems. A lot of them are worried about their studies and their exams; some want help with financial or legal problems, usually connected with renting flats and houses. Sometimes people want to talk about medical problems and for some reason don't want to see their doctor. The biggest problem, though, is loneliness. Universities are exciting places, but a lot of students find it difficult to make friends. They miss their families and friends and feel lost in this new environment. My job is to listen and try to understand what they're feeling. But of course I also give practical advice when it's needed.

'I've had two visits from students this morning. The first was a married student with a small child, and of course she can't take her child to classes. She asked me if I knew a good childcare centre. Then a young man came in, and I asked him what the matter was. He told me that he was lonely and unhappy. He asked me if other students felt the same and he asked me where he could go to meet people. He seemed very upset.'

7 Work in pairs.
Student A: Look at the police officer's report below and write each person's actual words. Start like this:
POLICE OFFICER: Is this your house?
JONES: Yes, it is.

Then compare your conversation with the one on page 122.
Student B: Turn to page 122. Read the conversation.

❝ I saw a man on a ladder at the back of Number 17, Sheep Street. His behaviour was a little strange, so I called to him. I asked him if that was his house. He said that it *was* his house, he couldn't find his key and he wanted to get in. I asked him if he had any identification. He said that his name was Mr Jones and his driving licence was in his car. As he climbed down the ladder, a neighbour came out of her house and asked me what the problem was. I said that Mr Jones wanted to get into his house. She looked at Jones and told me in a low voice that the people from Number 17 were on holiday. I arrested Jones and brought him to the police station. ❞

8 🔊 Listen and read. Sally Hall is Tom's teenage daughter. Sally's friend, Lucy, is upset and Sally's trying to help her. Answer the questions.
1 Why is Lucy upset?
2 What can Sally do to help?

SALLY: What's the matter?
LUCY: Oh, Sally, I've lost one of my earrings.
SALLY: Calm down. I'll help you look for it.
LUCY: But I've looked everywhere! Dad gave them to me and they're really expensive.
SALLY: Don't worry. It'll be all right. Now, why don't you tell me where you've been …

9 Match the functions with sentences from the conversation in Exercise 8.
1 – *I've lost one of my earrings.*
1 Say what the problem is.
2 Explain why the problem is serious.
3 Ask about the problem.
4 Reassure the person. Make a suggestion.
5 Calm the person. Offer to help.

10 🔊 Stress and intonation. Listen to these ways of reassuring people, and notice which words are stressed. Then listen and repeat.
Calm down! It's OK.
It'll be all right. Don't worry!
Everything's fine.

11 Work with a partner. Look at the pictures below. Write conversations using the same sequence of functions as the conversation in Exercise 8.

12 Now act out your conversation for the class. Be dramatic!

ENGLISH AROUND YOU

Development

SPEAKING

1 Look at the photograph of Christine Bahr above. Answer the questions.
1 What do you think her job is?
2 What does she do at work?

READING

2 Read about Christine and answer the questions.
1 What is her job?
2 Does she work with other women?
3 How long is her working day?

Christine Bahr is a firefighter. She works in San Carlos, California. She became a firefighter when she failed to get a job painting the Golden Gate Bridge in San Francisco. Some people think firefighting is a strange job for a woman, and in fact her fifty-nine colleagues are all men. It is a difficult job with long hours – twenty-four hours on duty, followed by twenty-four hours off duty.

3 Read about one day in Christine's life. Answer the questions.
1 Did the day start in an unusual way?
2 Who was responsible for the vehicle and the equipment?
3 What did the team do before lunch?
4 What did they do back at the station?
5 What do you think happened next?

> It was just another Sunday at the station. Everything was normal and we expected to have a quiet day. I was the driver that day, so I checked the engine and made sure all the equipment was working. Then we all spent a few hours out on the streets testing hydrants. On the way back to the station we stopped and bought some food to cook for lunch. When we got back, we turned on the television to watch a football game. It was then that we heard the first reports of a major fire . . . .

LISTENING

4 Listen to part of an interview with Christine. You will hear the names of some local places. Before you listen, identify:
1 an inter-city road.   a) Berkeley
2 a way across a river.   b) Highway 101
3 a city street.   c) Bay Bridge
4 a city.   d) Broadway Terrace

Were you right about what happened next?

5 Listen to the second part of the interview with Christine. Number the events in the correct order.
They went into a child's room.
They started to go down the staircase.
They entered the house.
The room filled with smoke.
Christine saw some photographs of the family.
They climbed up a narrow staircase.

6 🔊 Listen to the second part of Christine's interview again. Choose the correct answers.
1. The fire was:
   a) on the ground floor.
   b) in the garden.
   c) in the kitchen.
   d) on the top floor.
2. There were photographs:
   a) in the child's bedroom.
   b) on the wall next to the stairs.
   c) in the parents' bedroom.
   d) in the kitchen.
3. What did Christine do with the photographs?
   a) She put them in the fire engine.
   b) She gave them to the family.
   c) She put them in the next-door yard.
   d) She left them on the wall.

WRITING

7 Work with a partner. Think about the building you are in now and write down what you should and shouldn't do if there is a fire. If you do not know, find out!
We should ...
We shouldn't ...

8 Imagine that you can save one thing in your home from a fire. Write a paragraph about what you would save and why.
The most important thing to me is my guitar. I've had it for a long time, and it belonged to my father. It's a beautiful instrument and impossible to replace, so I would save it in a fire.

Summary

FUNCTIONAL LANGUAGE

Reporting what someone said
They said (that) the briefcase wasn't there.
They told me (that) the briefcase wasn't there.

Reporting what someone asked
She asked me if I could help her.
He asked me what I wanted.

Asking about past experiences
Have you ever been in a flood?
Yes, I have.
What happened?/When was that?

Apologising for lateness
I'm (very/so) sorry I'm late.

Reassuring someone
Don't worry! It'll be all right.

Calming someone
Calm down!

GRAMMAR

Reported speech (statements)
DIRECT SPEECH
'He isn't here,' she said.
REPORTED SPEECH
She said (that) he wasn't there.
DIRECT SPEECH
'I don't eat meat,' she told me.
REPORTED SPEECH
She told me that she didn't eat meat.
She said that she didn't eat meat.
present tense ⟶ past tense
here ⟶ there
Pronouns and possessives sometimes change.

Say* and *tell
say (that) + clause
tell + object pronoun *(that)* + clause

Reported speech (questions)

DIRECT SPEECH	REPORTED SPEECH
'Can you help me?' she asked.	She asked me if I could help her.
'What do you want?' he asked.	He asked me what I wanted.

See the Grammar Reference section at the back of the book for more information.

101

14 Celebrations

Good times

Focus

- Celebrations
- Congratulations
- Wishing someone well
- Congratulating someone
- Adverbs: *yet, already*
- Further practice: present perfect simple

A On Your Wedding Day
B Congratulations! On the birth of your New Baby
C Here's the key to the door! HAPPY BIRTHDAY
D What did you achieve in your exams?
E GOOD LUCK in your New Home!

1 Look at the cards. Match the sentences with the cards.

1 – Card A

1 They've just got married.
2 She's just become an adult.
3 They've just had a baby.
4 They've just moved house.
5 He's just passed his exams.

2 Now match the cards with the messages inside.

1 ... Correct. Well done!

2 Congratulations and best wishes to you and the newest member of your family.

3 This greeting comes to wish you both
Much love along life's way
Surrounded by the love you share
On this, your happy day.
We look forward to celebrating your first anniversary!

4 Congratulations on your moving experience!

5 Make the most of life's opportunities ... and have a lot of fun!

3 Say which card (A–E) each of these people received.

1 We're going to Brazil for our honeymoon. Then we want to spend a few years working abroad. My husband's a journalist and I'm a photographer. He's already lived overseas, but I haven't travelled much yet.

2 It's strange really. When you're seventeen you can drive and perhaps you've already left school but everyone thinks of you as a child. Then suddenly when you're eighteen, you're an adult. I haven't celebrated yet, but I'm going to!

3 I've just had my second child. I'm glad she's a girl because our first child was a boy. We've already chosen her first name, Sarah, but we haven't decided on a middle name yet.

4 Those were the last exams of my life, I hope, and I'm leaving college now. Have I found a job yet? Well, I've applied for one or two, but I'm waiting to hear if I've got an interview.

5 We've already lived in three different places, but we rented them. For the first time, we're in our own home. It feels wonderful. We can do exactly what we like with it.

DISCOVERING LANGUAGE

4 Look at the texts in Exercise 3 again. Find sentences with *yet* and *already*. Are the rules below true or false? Correct the false statements.
1. Both words are used with the present perfect tense.
2. They are both used in affirmative statements.
3. *Yet* comes at the beginning of a sentence.
4. *Already* comes between *have/has* and the past participle.
5. Both words mean *before now*.

5 Now look at these newspaper announcements. Write sentences about the events, using *yet* and *already*.

Sue hasn't gone to Australia yet.

FAMILY ANNOUNCEMENTS

SUE
Have a wonderful time in Australia! We'll miss you. With love from all the family.

ROBERT
Well done on passing your exams.
Love from EMILY

JOHN
Good luck in tomorrow's match.
Love from Mum and Dad xx
GOOD LUCK

Special Occasion
CYRIL & IVY WARD
Much love on your Ruby Wedding Anniversary tomorrow. Best wishes from Janet and Tina.

Congratulations!
Pat and Mike
We are looking forward to your wedding next week.
Rachel and Ian.

RONALD
Very best wishes for your retirement. It was a great party! Everyone at BIS Records.

TOM
Congratulations on passing your test! Third time lucky!! From all your mates.
You've passed.

🔊 COMPARING CULTURES

6 Find these symbols on the cards and the announcements. Then answer the questions.
a key   hearts   bells   a horseshoe   rings   a stork
1. Which symbols mean:
a) good luck?   c) love?   e) a new baby?
b) independence?   d) a wedding?
2. Do you use the same symbols in your country? If not, what symbols do you use?

7 Work with a partner and list times when people in your country send cards. Who do you send cards to and who do you receive them from?

birthdays   *I send birthday cards to my family and close friends.*

8 📼 Stress and intonation. Listen to these expressions and underline the syllables that are stressed. Then listen and repeat.

Congratulations!   Happy Birthday!   Well done!
Good luck!   Have a wonderful time!

9 Ask your partner about a special happy event in his/her life. Write a newspaper announcement on a form like the one below. Use one of these expressions:

Congratulations (on ...)!   Well done (on ...)!
Happy birthday/anniversary!   Good luck!
Best wishes (for/on ...).

Then answer your partner's questions about a happy event in your own life.

10 Write a short letter to your partner. Thank your partner for the announcement and tell him/her a little more about the event in your life.

Leaving

1 Work in pairs. It's Julia's last week at MAP Advertising and James and Rita are planning a leaving party for her.

Student A: You are Rita and your partner is James. Look at the list below and ask your partner about his tasks. Then answer questions about your tasks.

Student B: You are James. Turn to page 122. Look at the list of tasks.

RITA: James, have you bought the drinks yet?
JAMES: Yes, I have. Have you invited everyone yet?
RITA: No, not yet. Well I've already invited everyone in the office and all the clients, but I haven't invited Karl yet.

Focus

- Parties
- Speeches and toasts

- Toasting someone
- Thanking someone
- Further practice: wishing someone well

- Further practice: present perfect simple, *yet*, *already*

Julia's party

Rita
Invite everyone
(office staff ✓ clients ✓
Karl ✗)
Order some food ✓
Borrow some cassettes ✗
Buy Julia's present ✗

James
Buy drinks
Move the furniture
Write a card for Julia
Ask Sally to answer
the phones.

2 📼 Tom is making a speech at Julia's leaving party. Listen and put the pictures above in the correct order. Then match the pictures with the sentences.
1 He is giving Julia a present.
2 He is asking everyone to drink a toast.
3 He is talking about Julia's time at MAP Advertising.

3 📼 Listen again and answer the questions.
1 How long has Julia been with MAP Advertising?
2 Has Tom enjoyed working with her?
3 What has Julia decided to do?
4 Has Tom asked her to stay?

📼 Listen again to the toast that ends Tom's speech. Write the missing words.

TOM: Now ..... Julia and her new life.
ALL: ..... Julia!

🌐 COMPARING CULTURES

4 Read this short article about 'toasting'. Do you toast people in your country? What exactly do you say in your language?

In Britain, we usually toast people at formal celebrations like engagements, weddings, anniversaries, important birthdays, and the opening of new buildings. Someone will say 'I'd like to propose a toast to …John and Alice', if it's a wedding. Then everyone picks up a glass, raises it in the air, and says 'To John and Alice!', before drinking. In a more informal situation, we usually just say 'Cheers!', 'Good luck!' or 'All the best!'

5 Work in pairs. After the toast, Julia made a short speech. Look at her notes and discuss what she actually said. Start like this:

Friends and colleagues, I'd like to thank you all for this wonderful party …

Student A: Now make the speech to your partner.
Student B: Help your partner when he/she has a problem.
Then change roles.

THANK YOU – party, present
SAD DAY – 5 years at MAP, like second home; colleagues now friends.
Special thanks to Tom, help and support. Learnt a lot.
HAPPY DAY – new job, new places, new friends.
MAP – new offices; me – new life
BEST WISHES – to MAP, move to the country; to everyone.
Thanks for everything.
TOAST – to MAP

6 Work in pairs. Imagine it is the end of term. Prepare a speech of thanks to your teacher. Write notes, practise the speech, and then give it.

7 The day after the party, Julia wrote a letter to her friends and colleagues at MAP Advertising. Read the letter below and answer the questions.
1 What is the purpose of the letter?
2 What did the MAP staff give her as a present?
3 Match these descriptions with the parts of the letter:
   a) Explain why you like the gift.
   b) Say 'thank you' again.
   c) Say why you are writing.
   d) End the letter.
   e) Say that you hope to keep in contact.

10th July

Dear All,

1 – I am writing to thank you for the wonderful book and CDs that you gave me yesterday.
2 – As you know, I love music, particularly jazz and blues. The book on Charlie Parker was an excellent choice.
3 – Thanks also for the lovely card and your kind words.
4 – I hope to see you all again soon.
5 – Best wishes,

Julia

8 Match the opening phrases of these letters with the endings.
1 Bank to client:
   Dear Ms Tomlinson
2 Child to grandmother:
   Dear Gran
3 James to Julia:
   Dear Julia
4 Reader to editor of newspaper:
   Dear Sir/Madam

a) Love
b) Yours faithfully
c) Yours sincerely
d) Best wishes

Why did Julia end her letter 'Best wishes'?

9 Write a letter of thanks for a present that you have received recently. Organise your letter in the same way as Julia's.

Development

READING

1 Read about wedding ceremonies in Britain. Label the picture below with words from the text. Then complete these sentences.
1. In Britain, you can choose between a ..... and a ..... wedding ceremony.
2. You cannot marry before your ..... birthday.
3. There have to be ..... people in the room: the bride and groom, the registrar, and ..... .

Weddings

Seven out of ten people in Britain get married at some time in their lives, and there are two ways to get married. You can have a religious wedding ceremony (Christian, Muslim, Hindu, etc.) in a place that is registered for marriages, or a registrar can marry you in a civil ceremony without any religious content.

It is quite easy to arrange a civil ceremony. You can get a special licence and get married in about three days. The bride and groom are usually over eighteen, but people can marry at sixteen with their parents' permission. You need two witnesses at the ceremony who are over eighteen and who speak and understand English. There are no rules about clothes, so the bride and groom can wear anything. They can also choose their own music – even pop music. Some people like to read or listen to poetry, but most people only use the legal words of the ceremony. Whatever sort of ceremony people have, there is usually a reception afterwards. This is a party, often with a meal, for family and friends.

2 Find sentences in the text with *get married* and *marry*. What differences are there in the use of the two verbs?

SPEAKING AND WRITING

3 Work with a partner. Discuss the rules for marriage in your country, and compare them with what you now know about Britain.

Write sentences about:
- the types of ceremony.
- how old you have to be to get married.
- the people who have to be at the wedding ceremony, and the other people who come.
- what happens after the ceremony.
- the clothes that people wear at weddings.

In my country, all weddings are religious ceremonies . . .

LISTENING

4 Norman Stevens is a registrar at Kensington and Chelsea Register Office in London. Listen and answer the questions.
1. How long has he been a registrar?
2. How many couples has he married?
3. What is the largest number of couples that he has married in one day?

106

WRITING

5 Read this informal invitation. Complete Sarah's reply.

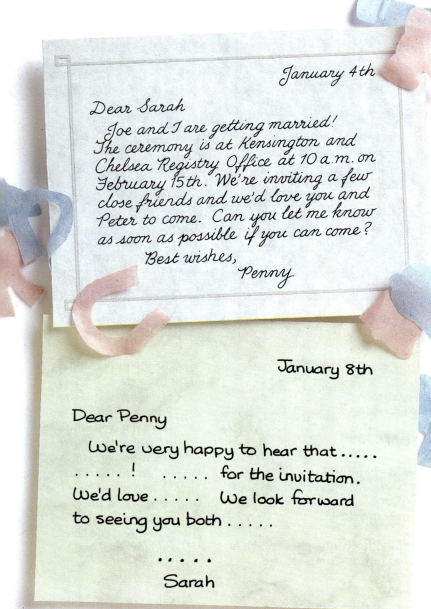

January 4th

Dear Sarah
Joe and I are getting married! The ceremony is at Kensington and Chelsea Registry Office at 10 a.m. on February 15th. We're inviting a few close friends and we'd love you and Peter to come. Can you let me know as soon as possible if you can come?
  Best wishes,
    Penny

January 8th

Dear Penny
  We're very happy to hear that . . . . .
. . . . . ! . . . . . for the invitation.
We'd love . . . . . We look forward to seeing you both . . . . .

    . . . . .
      Sarah

6 Write a short note like Penny's to your partner. Imagine you are having a party to celebrate an occasion like an engagement or an eighteenth birthday. Organise the note like this:
1 Explain the reason for the celebration.
2 Say where and when the party is.
3 Invite your partner.
4 Ask for a reply to the invitation.

UNIT FOURTEEN

Summary

FUNCTIONAL LANGUAGE

Wishing someone well for the future
Good luck (with your exams)!
All the best!

Wishing someone well now
Happy Birthday!
Happy Anniversary!

Congratulating someone
Congratulations (on passing your driving test)!
Well done!

Toasting someone
Here's to Julia/your future happiness!
Cheers!/All the best!
I'd like to propose a toast to Julia!

GRAMMAR

Adverbs: *already*, *yet*
I've *already* done it.
I haven't done it *yet*.
Have you done it *yet*?

See the Grammar Reference section at the back of the book for more information.

15 In the future

Predictions

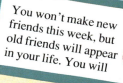
Weather forecasts — Tomorrow will be warm and sunny.

Horoscopes — You won't make new friends this week, but old friends will appear in your life. You will

Crystal balls — You will have serious problems.

Data analysis — The company won't make a profit until June.

Tea leaves — A visitor will arrive at your house.

Opinion polls — The Conservatives will win 32 per cent of the vote.

Focus

- Means of prediction
- Weather and weather forecasts

- Predicting
- Predicting with differing degrees of certainty
- Expressing hopes for the future
- Giving reactions: *I hope/think so. I hope not/I don't think so.*

- *Will* + infinitive for prediction
- Adverbs of degrees of certainty: *perhaps, probably, definitely, certainly*
- Irregular comparative and superlative adjective: *less, least*
- Further practice: superlative adjectives

1 Look at the different ways of predicting the future above and say what you think of them.
A: Are crystal balls accurate?
B: I think so./I don't think so./Of course not!/ I don't know.
A: Do you believe in their predictions?
B: Yes, I do./No, not at all./It depends.

↻ COMPARING CULTURES

2 Discuss ways of predicting the future.
1 Do people in your country use any of the methods above?
2 What other methods do they use?
3 How do you predict changes in your life?

3 📼 Listen to an interview with a young person. She is making predictions about her future. Complete the sentences with *will* or *won't*.
1 She probably ..... get a job.
2 She ..... certainly move out of her parents' house.
3 Perhaps she ..... move to a different part of the country.
4 She ..... probably get married in the next five years.
5 She definitely ..... have children immediately.
6 She doesn't think she ..... travel abroad.

Which adverbs mean that she is sure about her prediction?
probably   certainly   perhaps   definitely

DISCOVERING LANGUAGE

4 Study the sentences in Exercise 3.
1 Is *will* used here to refer to:
   a) what we *know* about the future?
   b) what we *believe* about the future?
2 Make rules about the position of the adverbs. Do they usually come before or after *will* and *won't*?

5 Ask your partner about future changes in his/her life and then write sentences.
A: Do you think you'll travel abroad?
B: I think so./ I don't think so./ I hope so./I hope not./ Perhaps./Probably./ Definitely.

6 Read these facts about the weather. Work with a partner to complete the chart below.

The highest temperatures	Dallol, Ethiopia
The lowest temperatures	....
The most sun	....
The least sun	....
The most rain	....
The least rain	....
The strongest winds	....
The most fog	....

WORLD WEATHER FACTS

The driest place Arica, in the north of Chile, has less than 0.1 mm of rain each year.

The foggiest place There is fog in some places on the Newfoundland coast of Canada for an average of 120 days a year.

The sunniest place In Yuma, Arizona, in the United States, the sun shines 90 per cent of the time.

The hottest place The average temperature in Dallol, Ethiopia, is 34°C.

The wettest place Tutunendo, Colombia, has an average of 11700 mm of rain every year.

The windiest place In parts of Antarctica, winds often reach 320 km an hour.

The coldest place The average temperature in one area of Antarctica is -58°C.

The cloudiest place For 182 days every year there is no sunshine at the South Pole because clouds cover the area.

7 Complete the chart with nouns from Exercise 6.

ADJECTIVE	NOUN
foggy	fog
sunny	.....
rainy (wet)	.....
windy	.....
cloudy	.....

8 The symbols below are used by the British Meteorological Office on their weather maps. Match the symbols with their meanings.

A – 6
1 foggy   6 temperature above zero
2 rainy   7 temperature below zero
3 sunny   8 sunny intervals
4 snow   9 thunderstorms
5 cloudy   10 wind speed and direction

9 Look at tomorrow's weather map of Britain. Read the forecast. Are the words in italics correct? If not, correct them.

The forecast for noon today.
Temperatures will be generally *high* in Scotland and the north of England, but will be *below zero* in the rest of the country. There will be *heavy rain* in Scotland, moving into northern England later in the afternoon. Wales and the South West will be *cloudy with sunny intervals* and with winds of up to *ten miles an hour*. The rest of England will be *wet*. In Northern Ireland, temperatures will be *just above zero*. There will be be *rain and some snow* in inland areas.

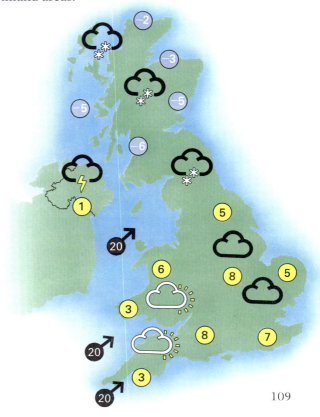

Focus

- Problems and solutions
- Stating consequences
- First conditional: If...

Problem solving

1 🎧 **Listen and read. Julia is talking to her friend Anna. Answer the questions.**

1 Why does Julia need advice?
2 What are her first two options?

JULIA: Anna, I still don't know what to do about my future. I need your help.
ANNA: OK. Well, why don't you tell me about the different options? Then we can talk about them.
JULIA: Yes, right. Well, it's not too late to change my mind and stay at MAP. If I stay, I won't have to look for another job. I'll also be able to work with people that I like. The second possibility is to go to Germany. Karl thinks that I'll be able to find a job there. If I go to Germany, I'll earn more money. On the other hand, I'll miss my friends.
ANNA: OK. Have you got any other options?

DISCOVERING LANGUAGE

2 Look at this pair of sentences. There is no basic difference in meaning.

If I go to Germany, I'll earn more money.
I'll earn more money if I go to Germany.

Now answer the questions.
1 Which tense follows *if*?
2 Which verb form is used in the other clause?

3 Look again at the conversation in Exercise 1. Find other first conditional *(if)* sentences and talk about Julia.
If Julia stays..., she...

4 Read Julia's list of options for the future. Add any other advantages and disadvantages that you can think of.

Stay at MAP Advertising
ADVANTAGES
- won't have to find new job
- continue to work with people I like

DISADVANTAGES
- have to leave London/move to the country/find a new flat

Find a job in Germany
ADVANTAGES
- live near Karl
- meet new people
- learn a new language

DISADVANTAGES
- have to leave London/move house
- miss friends

Get another job in London
ADVANTAGES
- be able to: stay in city/flat be with friends

DISADVANTAGES
- difficult to find job

Start my own company!
ADVANTAGES
- be my own boss
- work when I like
- see a new company grow (exciting!)

DISADVANTAGES
- expensive
- difficult to make new contacts
- have to work alone

5 Look at Julia's notes again and write about each option.
Her first option is to stay at MAP Advertising. If she stays at MAP Advertising, she won't have to find a new job...

6 🎧 **Stress and intonation. Listen. Does the speaker's voice go up or down at the end of each clause? What rule can you make?**

1 If she goes to Germany, she'll miss her friends.
2 She'll miss her friends if she goes to Germany.
3 If she stays at MAP, she'll have to leave London.
4 She'll have to leave London if she stays at MAP.

Now listen again and repeat the sentences.

7 Work with a partner. Discuss ways of solving the problems below. Use the first conditional to talk about the options.
1 *If we take away this match, there will be . . . triangles.*

1
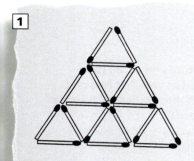
How can you take away three matches and leave a total of seven triangles?

2
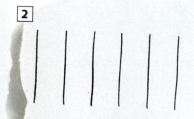
Draw these six lines. Then add five other lines and make nine.

3

The picture shows a small island in the middle of a deep lake. The lake is 300 metres across. There is a tree on the island, and another tree on the land. A woman wants to go from the land to the island. She can't swim. She has a rope that is 350 metres long. How can she reach the island?

4
A man wants to cross a ditch. The ditch is 3 metres wide and full of water. The man cannot swim. The only equipment that he can find is a pile of eight wooden planks. Each plank is about 2½ metres long. How can he cross the ditch?

5

A woman has to take a cat, a mouse and a large piece of cheese across a river in a small boat. She can only take one thing with her at a time. How can she take them all across without the cat eating the mouse and the mouse eating the cheese?

8 Work in small groups. Tell the group about a real or invented problem in your life. Ask for advice and discuss the different options.

9 📼 Listen to a conversation between Julia and James. Answer the questions below.

1 What is Julia going to do?
2 What does James hope for his future?
3 How does Julia feel about marriage?

ENGLISH AROUND YOU

I'll clear the table if you wash the dishes.

111

Development

SPEAKING

1 Read this old British saying about the weather. Look up any words you don't know in a dictionary.

> *Red sky at night, shepherd's delight.*
> *Red sky in the morning, shepherd's warning.*

This saying means that if the sky is red at sunset, the next day will be dry; if the sky is red at sunrise, it will rain.

Write down as many sayings about the weather as you can in your own language. Choose one and explain it to your partner in English.

READING

2 Read the article below about one system of forecasting and presenting the weather. Are these sentences true or false? Correct the false ones.

1. Television weather forecasts are more popular than news programmes.
2. BBC forecasters are professional presenters, not meteorologists.
3. Weather forecasts are recorded in advance.
4. Forecasts depend on observations.
5. Forecasters use computers to make predictions.
6. The presenters speak from memory.
7. Most television viewers listen carefully and remember what they hear.

LISTENING

3 Before you listen to a television weather forecast, match these cities to the areas they are in.

a) Moscow   c) Brussels
b) Beirut   d) Rome

1 Northern Europe
2 Southern Europe
3 Eastern Europe
4 the Eastern Mediterranean

4 Choose a city from Exercise 3. Listen to the forecast and make notes on the weather a) today and b) tomorrow.

The world of sunny intervals and scattered showers

In Britain, just after the main television news programmes, audience figures rise. It's weather forecast time. The BBC broadcasts forty-four live forecasts a day, 433 hours of weather a year, using forecasters from the Meteorological Office. The Met. Office makes predictions about the weather seven days in advance. These are based on observations from the ground, from satellites and from radar. The observations are stored in a computer that can do up to 4,000 million calculations a second.

In Britain the weather is news. A television weather forecast often begins with an interesting fact – the town with the top temperature of the day or the place with the most rain. 'The public like that kind of information,' say senior forecaster Bill Giles. The BBC forecasters are professional meteorologists, but they do not have an easy job. They are the only presenters on television who do not use a script, and they cannot see the map that they are describing. Viewers are often critical, especially of female presenters. One woman left her job after rude letters and press reports about her clothes.

The British talk about the weather more than almost any other subject, so it is a surprise to discover that seventy per cent of television viewers cannot remember what they saw on the weather forecasts. 'What happens is that people like watching and hearing the forecasts, but they probably only take real notice when they need to – when they're going on holiday or wondering what the weather will be like for the tennis at Wimbledon,' says one forecaster. 'Or, of course, when we make mistakes!'

WRITING

5 Either write a weather forecast for one of the places in Exercise 3 or find information about tomorrow's weather for your country and write a weather forecast in English.

READING AND SPEAKING

6 Read about Mr Foggitt's way of forecasting the weather. Which of these sentences is true for a) Mr Foggitt, and b) The Meteorological Office?

1. Information comes from watching animals and plants.
2. Information comes from satellites and radar.
3. Forecasts are short-term.
4. Forecasts are long-term.

No surprises for Foggitt

While Met. Office computers only give short-term forecasts seven days in advance, the amateur weather forecaster Bill Foggitt predicts much further into the future. He watches the animals and the plants around his house and bases his predictions on their behaviour. If flies are slow and lazy, it will rain. If garden spiders spin long webs, there will be dry, calm weather. And if his black cat runs madly around the kitchen, there will be high winds. How animals and plants sense future weather is a mystery. 'We need some serious scientific research,' says Mr Foggitt.

Summary

FUNCTIONAL LANGUAGE

Giving opinions
I (don't) think (that) he'll come.
Will he come?
I think so./I don't think so./Of course not!

Expressing hopes for the future
She hopes (that) she'll get married.
She hopes (that) she won't have children.
Will she get married? She hopes so.

Making predictions
It will rain tomorrow.
It won't snow.

Saying things with degrees of certainty
She will certainly/definitely/probably get a job.
Perhaps she'll get a job.
She probably won't get a job.

Expressing the consequences of possible actions
If I go to Germany, I'll earn more money.
I won't lose my friends if I stay here.

GRAMMAR

Will: predictions
AFFIRMATIVE
I/you/he/she/it/we/they *will* + infinitive
NEGATIVE
I/you/he/she/it/we/they *will not* + infinitive
SHORT FORMS
will ⟶ 'll
will not ⟶ won't
INTERROGATIVE
Will I/you/he/she/it/we/they + infinitive?

The first conditional
CLAUSE 1	CLAUSE 2
If + present simple,	(*will/ won't* + infinitive)
(*will/ won't* + infinitive)	*if* + present simple

Short answers: *hope/ think*
I hope so.   I think so.
I hope not.   I don't think so.

Adverbs
certainly   definitely   probably   perhaps

Irregular comparative/ superlative adjective
little–less–the least

See the Grammar Reference section at the back of the book for more information.

UNITS 13–15

Progress check 5

Vocabulary

1 Match each verb with a noun that can follow it.

climb – *a staircase*

1 move   a) a toast
2 pass   b) an exam
3 send   c) house
4 call   d) an anniversary
5 drink   e) a card
6 celebrate   f) a solicitor

2 Look at the map below and complete these sentences.

The ..... in Lyons is 17°C.
The temperature in Lyons is 17°C.

1 It is ..... and ..... in northern France today.
2 It is ..... in Paris and central areas.
3 Some ..... is falling in the Alps.
4 There is thick ..... on the Atlantic coast.
5 It is ..... in the south-west.
6 The ..... part of France today is on the south coast around Nice.

3 Complete the text below with these words.

bride   registrar   wedding   get married
honeymoon   reception   get engaged   husband

In Britain, people often (1) ..... some time before they (2) ..... . In civil wedding ceremonies, the official is called the (3) ..... . After the (4) ....., the family usually give a party, or (5) ....., for the (6) ..... and her new (7) ..... . Then the newly-married couple leave their guests and go away on their (8) ..... .

Grammar and functions

4 Complete the conversation.

A: (1) ..... a break-in?
B: Yes, I have.
A: (2) ..... ?
B: Oh, it was last year, in September. I felt awful.
A: (3) ..... ?
B: Well, we went out for the evening and when we came back we found the back door open. They took the video recorder, the television and the computer.

5 Complete these sentences. Report what A said to B.

A: 'I'm at home.'
B to C: *He said he was at home.*

1 A: 'There's something wrong with my leg.'
  B to C: 'He told .....'
2 A: 'I can't find Tom.'
  B to C: 'She said .....'
3 A: 'Your tickets aren't here.'
  B to C: 'He said .....'
4 A: 'I don't enjoy jazz.'
  B to C: 'She told .....'
5 A: 'What do they want?'
  B to C: 'She .....'
6 A: 'Can you wait for me?'
  B to C: 'He .....'
7 A: 'How much is the red sweater?'
  B to C: 'She .....'

114

PROGRESS CHECK 5

6 Which of these expressions usually refer to:
a) a past event?
b) a future event?
c) a present event?

Congratulations! a)
Congratulations!   Happy anniversary!
Well done!   Good luck!   Have a wonderful time!
Happy Birthday!

7 Use the prompts to write Pat's predictions about next weekend.

my parents/visit me/definitely
My parents will definitely visit me.
1 my sister/come too/perhaps
2 she/not want to come/probably
3 we/have some coffee/definitely
4 we/go for a walk/perhaps
5 we/eat in a restaurant/probably
6 my parents/not leave until the next day/perhaps

8 Use the prompts to ask Pat questions about her parents' visit. Complete her answers with *so* or *not*.

parents/pay for meal?
✓ I hope .....
Will your parents pay for the meal?
I hope so.
1 parents/bring their dog?
   ✗ I hope .....
2 sister's boyfriend/come too?
   ✗ I don't think .....
3 they/come by car?
   ✓ I think .....
4 they/sleep at your house?
   ✓ I hope .....
5 you/tell them about your job offer?
   ✓ I think .....
6 you/ask their advice?
   ✗ I don't think .....

9 Look at Alan's options before he decided to go to Africa. Complete the first conditional sentences.

I'll be with Rosie if I stay in Brighton.
1 I'll .....   3 If I .....   5 If I .....
2 If I .....   4 I'll .....

Stay in Brighton – be with Rosie
                – continue to work at the hospital
                – not be able to travel
Leave Brighton – visit new places
                – make new friends
                – not have job security

Common errors

10 Correct the word order.

We went away ago four months.
We went away four months ago.
1 She already has found a job.
2 I haven't eaten yet anything.
3 Have you been ever to Brazil?
4 The sun most of the time shines.
5 We won't probably sell our flat.

11 Add one word to correct each sentence.

Best wishes the happy couple!
Best wishes to the happy couple!
1 Congratulations your new job!
2 Can I talk you about my problems?
3 I'd like to thank you this lovely present.
4 It will rain the south of Scotland.
5 We'll be able sleep late tomorrow.
6 My salary depends my exam results.

12 Correct these sentences.

A registrar will get married us.
A registrar will marry us.
1 She said me that she couldn't come.
2 He asked me what did I want.
3 I've left school three months ago.
4 Do you believe about horoscopes?
5 It will be snow in Scandinavia.

13 Find the spelling mistake in each sentence below and correct the spelling.

My husband had a bad acident. – *accident*
1 He repaired the breaks on my bicycle.
2 We're just checking the equipement.
3 I'm enjoying my independance.
4 They're thinking about mariage and children.
5 Lonelyness is a problem when young people leave home.

At the end of the Progress Check, look back at your mistakes and study the Grammar Reference section for further help.

Exercises for Student B

Unit 1 Special interests

EXERCISE 6
You and your partner each have two pictures. Ask and answer questions and put the four pictures in the correct order. Use the verbs and nouns to help you.

B: *What's the woman doing in your first picture? Is she . . . ?*
A: *She's . . .*

3   to hang
    to fall
    rope
    bridge
    river

4   to wear
    to tie
    harness
    ankle

Unit 2 Learning languages

EXERCISE 3
Answer and ask questions to complete the chart.
A: *How many people speak English?*
B: *Three hundred and fifty million.*

MOTHER TONGUE SPEAKERS (IN MILLIONS)			
English	350	Chinese	.....
Japanese	120	German	.....
Arabic	150	Portuguese	.....
Russian	150	Spanish	.....
Hindi	200	Bengali	.....

Now put the languages in order of the number of speakers.

Unit 2 After school

EXERCISE 3
Look at the list of courses available at the Community Education Centre. Choose a course and ask your partner:
a) when the course is.
b) what time the classes are.
c) how long the course is.
d) how much it costs.

Make notes. Thank your partner when you have all the information.

COMMUNITY EDUCATION CENTRE

Courses

- Cinema studies
- Family history
- Foreign cookery
- Intermediate Italian
- Jazz exercise for women
- Painting in watercolours
- Photography
- Problems with writing?
- Return to learn
- Rock guitar club

EXERCISES FOR STUDENT B

Unit 3 Travel arrangements

EXERCISE 4
Look at the list below. Answer your partner's questions. Give short answers.

A: Who's going to ...?
B: Paula is.
A: Is Paula going to ...?
B: Yes, she is./No, she isn't.

> Things to do:
> borrow the tent – Paula
> get passports – Paula + John
> buy the plane tickets – Penny
> change some money – John
> buy the sleeping bags – Tim
> find the guidebook – Penny

Unit 3 Travel arrangements

EXERCISE 8
You are Teresa. Answer your partner.

MARCO: I'm going to *Brighton at the weekend*. Would you like to come?
TERESA: Oh, yes. I'd love to.
MARCO: Oh, good. I'm going to catch the *ten o'clock train*. Is that OK?
TERESA: That's fine.
MARCO: Don't be late. It's the only *fast train*.
TERESA: Don't worry. I'll be there.
MARCO: Let's meet at *the ticket office* at half past nine. Or earlier at your flat?
TERESA: Er ... no, I'll see you at *the ticket office*.

Now change roles and use the information below to replace the phrases in italics.

> You're going to Glasgow on Sunday by plane. It's a non-stop flight and it leaves at 9.45 a.m. Arrange to meet in the airport café an hour before.

Unit 4 The right clothes

EXERCISE 6
You are the shop assistant. The picture shows the prices of clothes in your shop. When your customer tells you what he/she wants, remember to ask about size and about trying on the clothes.

Unit 5 Problems with vehicles

EXERCISE 8

Look at the chart. Answer your partner's questions about the laws for riding mopeds in the UK. Then complete the last column about your country.

A: *Do moped riders have to wear crash helmets in Britain?*
B: *Yes, they do.*
A: *Can they ride on motorways?*

	UK	YOUR COUNTRY
wear a crash helmet?	Yes	.....
have a driving licence?	Yes	.....
be sixteen years old?	Yes	.....
ride on motorways?	No	.....
ride on cycle paths?	No	.....
carry more than one person on the back?	No	.....

Unit 7 Getting to work

EXERCISE 4

Read the articles and match them with two of the pictures. Answer your partner's questions. Then ask questions about the journeys in the other pictures.

How ... ? How far ... ? How long ... ?
How much ... ?

C Jane Hatherall is an accountant. Every Monday morning she takes her car to work. In the car are the clothes that she needs during the week. She keeps them at the office. On the other days she runs to work. The four-mile journey takes forty-five minutes. She is hot and dirty when she arrives, but her company provides sports facilities so she has a swim and a shower and changes into her smart clothes. Then she is ready for work.

D Every day Paul Doyle roller-skates to his job at the Richmond Hill Hotel. He leaves his parents' home at 7.05 a.m. and arrives at work ten minutes later, a journey of four miles that takes forty minutes by bus. He leaves his uniform at work but carries a clean shirt in his backpack.

118

Unit 7 Getting to work

EXERCISE 8
Ask for directions to each of these famous places. Answer your partner's questions using the maps below.

Madame Tussaud's   the Hard Rock Café
Buckingham Palace   the Tate Gallery
Trafalgar Square

B: *Excuse me. How do I get to Madame Tussaud's?*
A: *What's the nearest underground station to Madame Tussaud's?*
B: *Er... I think the nearest station's Baker Street.*
A: *Right. Take the Central Line to Oxford Circus, then change to the Jubilee Line. Get off at Baker Street.*

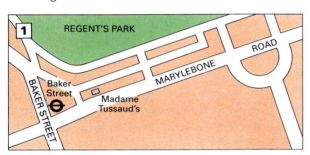

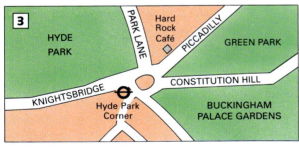

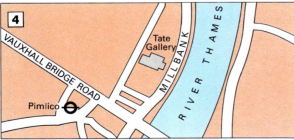

Unit 7 Development

EXERCISE 2
Look at the maps and answer your partner's questions.

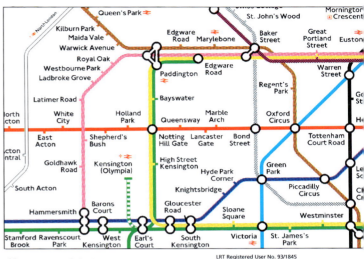

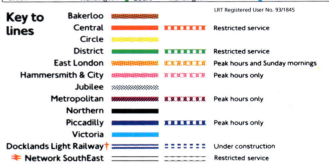

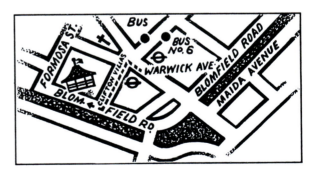

Unit 8 Shopping for food

EXERCISE 2
Look at the items on Teresa's shopping list that she has already got (✓) and answer your partner's questions.

A: How much ice cream has Teresa got?
B: She's got two litres.
A: How many carrots has she got?
B: …

Now answer your partner's questions about the other things that Teresa needs.

A: What else does she need?
B: She needs some flour.
A: How much flour does she need?
B: …

Shopping list
2 litres of ice cream ✓
1 kilo of carrots ✓
1 kilo of flour
a small bottle of shampoo
a large pizza
a bottle of olive oil
a box of chocolates (500g) ✓
a tin of peas
a cucumber
2kg lamb ✓
2 loaves of bread
3 litres of milk ✓
6 rolls of toilet paper

Unit 8 Shopping for food

EXERCISE 8
You are the shop assistant. Look at the pictures and answer your partner's questions.

Unit 10 Giving details

EXERCISE 5
Answer your partner's questions about the objects below. Then ask questions and identify the three objects in your partner's pictures.

1 a blanket

2 a frying pan

3 a chocolate wrapper

Unit 10 Giving details

EXERCISE 8
You are selling the items below. Your partner phones you about them. Answer his/her questions.

B: 865412.
A: Hello. I saw your advertisement at the newsagent's. Could you give me some information about the carpet?
B: Certainly. What would you like to know?
A: ...

> Tel 865412
> FOR SALE
> Large carpet – £150 (4m wide, 6m long, dark grey nylon; nearly new)
> Colour TV – £50 (Philips, 45cm x 45cm x 42cm; screen 40cm wide; black case; remote control
> Computer desk – £85 (grey and white metal with wheels; 69cm high x 100cm wide x 70cm deep; special shelves for printer and paper)

Now change roles. Look at the advertisement on the right. Phone your partner and ask for more information. Make notes.

> **FOR SALE**
> Tent £35
> Portable CD player £60
> 3 shelves £10 each
> **Telephone 422307**

Unit 10 Development

EXERCISE 2
You are at the Lost Luggage Office at an airport. You can't find your suitcase. Describe your suitcase (right) to the airport official.

Unit 11 Development

EXERCISE 4
You want to do body-conditioning classes next summer. Ask about dates, days, times and the cost of classes. Make notes and then compare the information you have with the information on pages 86–87. Did your partner give you the correct information?

Unit 13 Asking for help

EXERCISE 7
Read the conversation. Complete the police officer's report of the incident, and then compare your report with the one on page 99.

POLICE OFFICER:	Is this your house?
JONES:	Yes, it is. I can't find my key, and I want to get in.
POLICE OFFICER:	Have you any identification?
JONES:	My name is Mr Jones, and my driving licence is in my car.
NEIGHBOUR:	What's the problem?
POLICE OFFICER:	Mr Jones wants to get into his house.
NEIGHBOUR:	(*in a low voice*) The people from Number 17 are on holiday!

❛ I saw a man on a ladder at the back of Number 17, Sheep Street. His behaviour was a little strange, so I called to him. I asked ..... . He said ..... . I asked ..... . He said ..... . As he climbed down the ladder, a neighbour came out of her house and asked ..... . I said ..... . She looked at Jones and told ..... . I arrested Jones and brought him to the police station. ❜

Unit 14 Leaving

EXERCISE 1
It's Julia's last week at MAP Advertising and James and Rita are planning a leaving party for her.

You are James and your partner is Rita. Look at the list and answer your partner's questions. Ask about Rita's tasks.

RITA: James, have you bought the drinks yet?
JAMES: Yes, I have. Have you invited everyone yet?
RITA: No, not yet. Well, I've already invited everyone in the office and all the clients, but I haven't invited Karl yet.

Julia's party

Rita
Invite everyone
(office staff / clients / Karl)
Order some food
Borrow some cassettes
Buy Julia's present

James
Buy drinks ✓
Move the furniture ✗
Write a card for Julia ✓
Ask Sally to answer the phones ✗

Grammar reference

This is a summary of the grammar in this book. If a grammar area is difficult for you, read that part of the Grammar Reference. Then look back at the unit in the Students' Book or do some practice exercises in your Workbook.

1 Nouns

Nouns are words which refer to people (*manager*), things (*cassette*), places (*London*), feelings and ideas (*love*).

1.1 Countable nouns

Countable nouns refer to people or things that you can count. They have a singular and a plural form: *a computer – two computers*. If the noun is the subject of a verb, the verb is also singular or plural: *The girl **is** my sister. The boys **are** my brothers.*

1.2 Uncountable nouns

Uncountable nouns refer to things or ideas that you cannot count. They have no plural form and are not used with the indefinite article (*a/an*): *food*. If the noun is the subject of a verb, the verb is singular: *The soup **is** on the table.* Some nouns have countable and uncountable forms: *Two **teas**, please.* (two cups of tea = countable) *Would you like some **tea**?* (some tea = uncountable)

2 Quantities

2.1 Some/any (Unit 8)

We use *some* and *any* with plural nouns and uncountable nouns. They refer to a number of things or a quantity of something which is not specific.

a We usually use *some* in affirmative statements: *There are **some** visitors in the school.* We sometimes use *some* in questions, requests and offers when we think the answer is *yes*: *Can I have **some** orange juice, please?*

b We usually use *any* in negative statements and in questions when we have no expectation about the answer: *I haven't got **any** money. Is there **any** tea?*

2.2 A few/a little/many/much/a lot (of) (Unit 8)

We use these words to refer to quantities of things.

a *A few* and *a little* refer to small quantities. *A few* is used with plural nouns: ***A few*** *students. A little* is used with uncountable nouns: ***A little*** *cheese.*

b *Many* and *much* refer to large quantities. They are usually used in questions and negative statements. *Many* is used with plural nouns: *How **many** children have you got? Much* is used with uncountable nouns: *How **much** meat did you buy?*

c *A lot of* refers to large quantities. We usually use it in affirmative statements with plural or uncountable nouns: ***A lot of*** *people are coming to our party.*

d We can also use these words without a noun: *How much money have you got? I haven't got **much**./I've got **a little**./I've got **a lot**./How many chairs are there? There aren't **many**./There are **a few**./There are **a lot**.*

3 Pronouns

We use pronouns in place of a noun when it is not necessary or possible to be more specific about the identity of a person or thing.

3.1 Subject pronouns

These are the subject of a verb. They usually come before the verb. The subject pronouns are:
I   you   he   she   it   we   you   they

3.2 Object pronouns (Unit 6)

These are the object of a verb. They usually follow the verb. The object pronouns are:
me   you   him   her   it   us   you   them

3.3 Indefinite pronouns: *Some(one), any(thing), no(one), every(thing)* (Unit 10)

We use these indefinite pronouns when it is not important who or what we are referring to.

a Indefinite pronouns can be used in subject or object positions. They are used with singular verb forms: *Everyone **likes** her. Someone's coming.*

b Pronouns that begin with *some-* usually follow the rules for *some* in 2.1a above.

c Pronouns that begin with *any-* usually follow the rules for *any* in 2.1b above.

d Words that begin with *no-* are used with an affirmative verb form. *I can see **nothing*** means the same as *I can't see **anything**.*

3.4 Possessive pronouns (Unit 10)

We use possessive pronouns in place of possessive adjectives and nouns: *The blue book is **mine*** means the same as *The blue book is **my book***. The forms are:

mine   yours   his   hers   its   ours   yours   theirs

4 Adjectives

Adjectives give information about a person or thing.

4.1 Order of adjectives (Units 4, 10)

a Adjectives usually come before a noun or after the verb *to be*: *It's a **red** dress. It's **red**.*

b We usually list adjectives in the following order:
1 adjectives that express opinions
2 adjectives that refer to other, factual qualities (e.g. size, age)
3 adjectives that describe colour
4 adjectives that describe material

*It's a **beautiful**, **long**, **black**, **leather** coat.*

c Three or more adjectives are usually listed with commas. When there are only two adjectives, a comma is usually unnecessary: *a **big blue** boat*. If both describe colours or materials, we put *and* between them: *a **red and green** carpet*.

d When there are two or more adjectives after a verb, and they are not followed by a noun, we usually put *and* between the last two adjectives: *His beard was **long**, **thick and black**.*

4.2 Comparative and superlative adjectives (Units 3, 4)

We use comparative adjectives to compare two or more people or things. The adjective is often followed by *than* to show who or what you are comparing the subject with: *James is **older than** Clare and Rachel.*

We use superlative adjectives to compare a person or thing with all others in a particular category. *The* usually comes before the superlative adjective: *James is **the youngest** person at MAP.*

a Comparative and superlative forms of a short (one or two syllable) adjective are:
Comparative adjective = + *er* (*clean – clean**er***)
Superlative adjective = + *est* (*cheap – cheap**est***)
Some short adjectives form comparatives and superlatives in other ways:
- Adjective ending in a vowel and a consonant = repeat the consonant + *er/est* (*fat, fatter, fattest*)
- Adjective ending in e = + *r/st* (*late*, lat*er*, lat*est*)
- Adjective ending in y = change y to i + *er/est* (*early, earlier, earliest*)

b Long adjectives (usually three syllables or more) form the comparative and superlative like this: *the + more/most* + adjective (*beautiful*, **more** *beautiful*, **most** *beautiful*)

c Some two syllable adjectives can use the short or long form (*friendl**ier***, **more** *friendly*; *friendl**iest***, **most** *friendly*).

d Some irregular forms are: *good – **better** – **best** bad – **worse** – **worst**   little – **less** – **least**.*

4.3 Adjectives with *too* and *enough* (Unit 4)

a *Too* + adjective indicates a problem: *This coat's **too short**. (I want a longer one.)*

b Adjective + *enough* has a positive meaning: *This coat is **long enough**. (It is the right length.)*

5 Verbs

Verbs and verb phrases tell us about actions or states.

5.1 The present simple (Unit 1)

USES
We use the present simple to talk about:

a a present habit or routine. It is often used with adverbs of frequency: *They **play** tennis at weekends.*

b A situation in the present that continues for a long time: *She **lives** in London.*

FORMS

a Study the forms of the verb:
*I/you/he/she/it/we/they work**ed**.*
*He/she/(it)/**works**/here.*
***Do** I/you/we/they/**live**/here?*
***Does** he/she/(it)/**live**/here?*
*I/you/we/they **do not (don't)**/swim/here.*
*He/she/(it) **does not (doesn't)**/swim/here.*

b Some verbs form the third person singular or the present simple in other ways:
- verbs ending in consonant + y = y̶ + *ies*   (*cry – cries*)
- verbs ending in *o, ch, sh, ss, x, zz* = + *es*   (*go – goes*)

5.2 The present progressive (Unit 1)

USES
We use the present progressive (or present continuous) to talk about:

a A present and temporary activity: *Susan **is working** at home today.*

b Fixed future plans, often with a future time adverbial: *I **am going** on holiday next Tuesday.*

FORMS

a Study the form of the present progressive: *to be* + present participle (*ing* form): *He's **playing** in the garden. **Are** you **playing** too? I'm **not playing** with him.*

b We form the present participle in these ways:
- Infinitive + *ing*: *walk – walking*
- Infinitive ending in e = e̶ + *ing*   (*dance – dancing*)
- one syllable infinitive ending in one vowel and one consonant = + the same consonant again + *ing* (*stop – stopping*)

- two or more syllable infinitive ending in one vowel and one consonant, with stress on the last syllable = + the same consonant again + *ing* (*begin – beginning*)
- two or more syllable infinitive ending in one vowel and one *l* = + *l* + *ing* (*travel – travelling*)

5.3 Stative verbs (Unit 1)

Dynamic verbs (e.g. *go, play*) refer to actions, events or processes and are used in progressive and simple verb forms. Stative verbs refer to states or situations that are not usually within our control.

We do not usually use these verbs in the progressive form: *I **understand** what you are saying*. Some common stative verbs are: understand want know like love hate believe see hear prefer

5.4 The past simple (Unit 2)

USE

We use the past simple to talk about an action, event or state at a specific time in the past. It is often used with a past time adverbial: *My parents **arrived** yesterday*.

FORMS

a Study the affirmative form of regular verbs:
- Infinitive + *ed* (*work – work**ed***)
  *I/you/he/she/it/we/they work**ed**.*
- Infinitive ending in *e* = +*d* (*like – lik**ed***)
- Infinitive ending in *y* = ̶y̶ + *ied* (*hurry – hurr**ied***)
- Infinitive ending in one consonant = repeat the last consonant + *ed* (*stop – stopp**ed***)

b Study the affirmative forms of some irregular verbs:

INFINITIVE	PAST	INFINITIVE	PAST
be	was/were	meet	met
become	became	pay	paid
begin	began	put	put
bring	brought	read	read
build	built	say	said
buy	bought	see	saw
come	came	sell	sold
do	did	send	sent
drink	drank	shut	shut
drive	drove	sleep	slept
eat	ate	speak	spoke
find	found	spend	spent
get	got	stand	stood
give	gave	take	took
go	went	teach	taught
have	had	tell	told
keep	kept	think	thought
know	knew	understand	understood
leave	left	wear	wore
make	made	write	wrote

c We form questions with *did* and the infinitive (without *to*): ***Did** you **like** it?*

d We form negative statements with *did not* (short form = *didn't*) and the infinitive: *I **didn't see** any friends.*

5.5 Imperatives (Unit 6)

We use imperative forms to give instructions or advice. The form is the same as the infinitive without *to*: ***Stop!*** We form the negative with *do not* (short form = *don't*) and the infinitive without *to*: ***Don't smoke** here, please!*

5.6 *Going to* (Unit 2)

USE

We use *going to* to talk about plans or intentions for the future: *We're **going to** fly to Pisa tomorrow*.

FORMS

Study the form of structures with *going to*: *to be* + *going to* + infinitive: *She's **going to** study French. **Are** they **going to study** French? We **aren't going to study** French.*

5.7 The present simple passive (Unit 10)

USE

We often use a passive construction if we do not know the identity of the person or thing performing an action, or if this information is unimportant. The subject is the person or thing that the action affects: *Things **are** frequently **stolen** from this café*. This is different from the active sentence, in which the subject performs the action: *People frequently steal things from this café*.

FORM

We form the present simple passive from the correct present tense form of the verb *to be* + the past participle: *It's **made** of wood. **Is** it **made** of wood?*

In this book the passive is only used in one context: *What's it **made** of? It's **made** of (metal and glass)*.

5.8 The present perfect simple (Units 11, 12, 14)

USES

The present perfect is used to talk about:

a something that happened at an unspecified time in the recent or distant past: *The match **has finished**.*

b a situation that began at a point in the past and continues to the present moment: *She **has been** here for ten years.*

FORMS

We form the present perfect simple from the verb *to have* + the past participle.

a Study the forms of the present perfect simple: *I**'ve seen** that film. **Have** you **seen** it? She **hasn't seen** it.*

b Regular verbs form past participles by adding *ed* to the infinitive (*walk – walk**ed***).

c Study the past participles of some irregular verbs:

INFINITIVE	PAST PARTICIPLE	INFINITIVE	PAST PARTICIPLE
be	been	meet	met
become	become	pay	paid
begin	begun	put	put
bring	brought	read	read
build	built	say	said
buy	bought	see	seen
come	come	sell	sold
do	done	send	sent
drink	drunk	shut	shut
drive	driven	sleep	slept
eat	eaten	speak	spoken
find	found	spend	spent
get	got	stand	stood
give	given	take	taken
go	gone (/been)	teach	taught
have	had	tell	told
keep	kept	think	thought
know	known	understand	understood
leave	left	wear	worn
make	made	write	written

5.8.1 *For/since* (Unit 12)

We often use *for* and *since* with present perfect verb forms to specify the duration of a situation that started in the past and continues now. *For* refers to a period of time: *I've been here **for** an hour*. *Since* emphasises when the period began: *I've been here **since** last Saturday*.

5.8.2 *Yet/already/just* (Units 11, 14)

We often use these words with present perfect verb forms.

a *Yet* is used in questions and negative sentences to refer to the period of time until now. We usually put *yet* at the end of a sentence or clause: *Has she arrived **yet**?*

b We usually use *already* in affirmative statements to emphasise that something has happened. We put it between *have/has* and the past participle or at the end of a sentence: *When are you going to phone James? I've **already** phoned him! / I've phoned him **already**!*

c *Just* emphasises that something happened very recently. We usually put it between *have/has* and the past participle: *They've **just** left.*

5.8.3 *Ever/never* (Unit 12)

We often use *ever* and *never* with present perfect tense verbs. They come before the past participle. We use *ever* in questions to refer to the whole of a person's experience: *Have you **ever** been to India?* We use *never* with affirmative verb forms: *They have **never** been to Africa.*

5.9 *Have to* (Unit 5)

USE

We use *have to* to talk about the necessity or importance of doing something: *We **have to** catch the 6.30 train.*

FORMS

a Study the form of structures with *have to*: *have* + infinitive (with *to*): *We **have to go** now. **Do** I **have to go**? He **doesn't have to go**.*

b We can use *have got to* in informal speech in place of the present tense of *have to*: *I've **got to go**.*

c The past simple form of *have to* is *had to*: *You **had to** go.*

5.10 Phrasal verbs (Unit 6)

The phrasal verbs in this book consist of a main verb (e.g. *turn*) and a particle (e.g. *on/off*). The meaning of the whole is often not the same as the meaning of its parts, so you have to learn the meaning of the whole verb. Phrasal verbs are common in spoken English and less common in writing, especially formal writing.

FORMS

In this book, most phrasal verbs are of one type:

a They are transitive, so are followed by an object: *He **turned up** the radio.*

b If the direct object is a pronoun, you put it between the main verb and the particle: *He **turned** it **on**.*

c If the direct object is a noun, you put it between the main verb and the particle or after the particle: *He **turned** the television **on**. He **turned on** the television.*

6 Modal verbs

6.1 *Can* and *could* (Units 2, 5)

USES

Can and *could* are used:

a To talk about a person's abilities: *I **can** drive a car.*

b To ask for something: *Can (Could) I have a cup of tea?* To express possibility: *I **can (could)** come tonight.* *Can* is also used to talk about permission: *You **can** go now. Can't* is used to talk about prohibition: *You **can't** park there.*

FORMS

a *Could* can express the past of *can* for ability. In other functions, *could* does not refer to the past. It is used in requests to be more polite: *Could you help me?* is more polite than *Can you help me?*

b *Can* and *could* are used with an infinitive (without *to*): *I/you/he/she/it/we/they **can/could dance**.*

c We form questions by putting *can/could* before the subject: *Can/Could he type?*

d We form negative statements by adding *not* (short form = *'t*) to *can*. (Note than *cannot* is one word, not two.): *People **cannot/can't** understand my French.* The negative form of *could* is *could not* (short form = *couldn't*): *We **could not/couldn't** come.*

6.2 *Will* (Units 3, 15)

USES

In this book *will* is used to:

GRAMMAR REFERENCE

a Express a decision that you make now about the future: *I'll go by car. No I won't, I'll fly.*
b Make predictions about the future: *It will rain tomorrow. It won't snow.*
c Make promises: *I'll be there on time. I won't be late.*

FORMS

a We form affirmative statements with *will* (short form = *'ll*) + infinitive without *to*: *We will ('ll) take the job.*
b We form questions by putting *will* before the subject: *Will they be friends?*
c We form negative statements by putting *not* between *will* and the infinitive (short form = *won't*): *It will not (won't) rain tomorrow.*

6.3 Should (Unit 9)

USES

In this book *should* is used to give advice and to say what is best.

FORMS

a We form affirmative statements with *should* + infinitive (without *to*): *You should see a doctor.*
b We form questions by putting *should* before the subject: *Should we take him to the doctor?*
c We form negative statements with *not* (short form = *n't*): *We should not/shouldn't stay here.*

7 Sentence structure

7.1 Verbs followed by gerunds and infinitives (Units 1, 2, 3)

Some verbs are followed by particular verb constructions.

a These verbs are usually followed by verb + *ing*: *stop, dislike, enjoy, finish, can't stand*: *I enjoy swimming.*
b These verbs are usually followed by an infinitive + *to*: *want, would like, would prefer, offer, learn, promise*: *I want to go to London so I can learn to speak English.*
c These verbs can be followed by either verb + *ing* or infinitive + *to*: *begin, start, intend, continue, like, prefer, hate, love, try*: *I prefer to walk to work, but Jane prefers cycling.*

7.2 Reported speech (Unit 13)

USES

We use reported speech to refer to a statement or question that we or another person made earlier.

DIRECT SPEECH: *'I'm going to London.'*
REPORTED SPEECH: *He said he was going to London.*

FORMS

a We use the verbs *say*, *tell* and other reporting verbs to report statements. *That* is often used to introduce the reported speech. *Tell* is always followed by an indirect object and then a clause of reported speech.

	VERB	OBJECT	CLAUSE
She	told	me	(that) she was late.

Say never takes an object before the clause of reported speech: *He said (that) it was raining.*

b We use *ask* to report questions. *Ask* is often followed by an indirect object: *They asked me what the time was.*
c After a present tense reporting verb, the tense of the verb in the reported speech does not change.
DIRECT SPEECH: *'I'm going to India.'*
REPORTED SPEECH: *She says that she is going to India.*
d When the reporting verb is in the past tense, we often have to change the tense of the verb in the direct speech when we report it. Other changes that are usually necessary are changes to pronouns, possessives and adverbs of place and time.

DIRECT SPEECH *'I love spaghetti.'*
REPORTED SPEECH *She told me (that) she loved spaghetti.*
DIRECT SPEECH *'I don't eat meat.'*
REPORTED SPEECH *He said (that) he didn't eat meat.*
DIRECT SPEECH *'What's your name?'*
REPORTED SPEECH *He asked me what my name was.*
DIRECT SPEECH *'Do you live here?'*
REPORTED SPEECH *I asked her if she lived there.*
DIRECT SPEECH *'Is he at work today?'*
REPORTED SPEECH *I asked if he was at work that day.*

e When we report questions, the report is not a question. The word order in a reported question is like the word order of a statement; the subject comes before the verb.

	SUBJECT	VERB	
I asked her if	she	lived	there.

7.3 Indirect questions (Unit 8)

USES

There is a general rule that one way to be more polite is to use more indirect language.

DIRECT: *What's the time?*
INDIRECT: *Can you tell me what the time is?*

The introductory phrase *Can you tell me ... ?* is a useful way of making questions more polite. Another phrase is *Do you know ... ?*: *Do you know when the bank opens?*

FORM

The phrase *Can you tell me ... ?* carries the grammatical question form, so you do not need another question form in the words that follow.

a To make a *wh* question more polite, use an introductory phrase + *wh* word + subject + verb: *Can you tell me where the bank is?*
b To make other questions more polite, use an introductory phrase + *if* + subject + verb: *Do you know if the bank is open?*

7.4 First conditional sentences (Unit 15)

USE

If is often used to refer to actions, events or situations that depend on other actions, events or situations. We often

127

use the first conditional to express a strong link between the condition in the *if* clause and the consequence: **If** she arrives before 7, we'll catch the 8 o'clock bus.

FORMS

a Conditional sentences have at least two clauses – the *if* (condition) clause, and the clause with the consequence.

b The consequence clause can also come first: *I'll give him the books if I see him.*

c A standard form of the first conditional is:

IF +	PRESENT TENSE CLAUSE, +	WILL CLAUSE	
If	I **see** him,	I'**ll give**	him the books.

7.5 Tag questions (Unit 9)

USES

The tag questions in this book are used to check something that you are not sure about or to confirm that something is true.

FORMS

a A tag question has two parts:

STATEMENT	QUESTION TAG
You are coming,	aren't you?

b The tense and person of the verb in the question tag are the same as the tense and person of the main verb.

c The tag is formed with an auxiliary or modal *(do, can, etc.)* and the same subject as the statement. **He is** going, **isn't he?**

d In this book, we look at one kind of question tag. If the main verb is affirmative, the verb in the question tag is negative. These questions expect the answer *yes*. If the main verb is negative, the verb in the question tag is affirmative. These questions expect the answer *no*.
It'**s** Polish, **isn't** it? Yes, it **is**.
It **isn't** Polish, **is** it? No, it **isn't**.

8 Adverbs

An adverb gives more information about when, how or where something happens.

8.1 Frequency (Unit 1)

USE

We use frequency adverbs to say *how often* something happens: They **often** visit Britain.

POSITION

a Frequency adverbs usually come before the main verb or after the verb *to be*: We **sometimes** eat out. They come after auxiliary and modal verbs (e.g. *can, have*): I can **never** work at home.

b *Sometimes* and *occasionally* can also come at the beginning or end of a sentence: **Sometimes** I sleep all weekend. I sleep all weekend **sometimes**.

c We can also put *usually* and *often* at the beginning of a sentence: **Usually/often** we go for a run before school.

8.2 Manner

USE
These adverbs tell you *how* something happens. They usually come after the object (or after the verb when there is no object).

FORMS

a Regular adverbs are formed by adding *ly* to an adjective: *dangerous – dangerously*
Some adverbs are formed in slightly different ways:
- adjective ending in *y* = ɤ + *ily* (*easy – easily*)
- adjective ending in *le* = ɫe + *ly* (*terrible – terribly*)
- adjective ending in *ic* = + *ally* (*automatic – automatically*)
(Note the exception: *public – publicly*)
- noun + *ly* (*month – monthly*)

b Irregular adverbs in this book include:
good – well   hard – hard   fast – fast

8.3 Time

These adverbs tell you *when* something happens. They usually come at the beginning or (more often) at the end of a clause or sentence: He was at home **yesterday**. **Yesterday** he was at home.

8.4 Sequence (Unit 6)

Some adverbs are used to describe a sequence of events or actions: **First** switch it on, **and then** wait a minute. **Next** insert a disk .... **Finally**, switch it off.

8.5 Degrees of certainty (Unit 15)

These adverbs are used to describe how probable or certain something is: He'll **definitely** come.

a In affirmative sentences, most adverbs come before the main verb but after an auxiliary: They **probably** ate at home. They have **probably** eaten.

b In negative sentences, most adverbs come before the auxiliary and the main verb: They **certainly** didn't go.

c *Perhaps* usually comes at the beginning of a sentence: **Perhaps** it will rain.

8.6 *Somewhere, everywhere, anywhere, nowhere* (Unit 10)

We use these indefinite adverbs of place when we are not referring to a specific place.

a We usually use *somewhere* and *everywhere* in affirmative statements: I've looked **everywhere**.
We also use them in questions, requests and offers when we think the answer is *yes*: Can I take you **somewhere**?

b We usually use *anywhere* in questions and negative sentences: Have you seen my bag **anywhere**?

c *Nowhere* usually occurs as a one-word answer to a question: Where have you been? **Nowhere.**